MULTIPLE
CHOICE

Praise for

MULTIPLE CHOICE

"Martha Singleton has once again given voice to parents, children, and educators with this brilliantly crafted and beautifully articulated guide to finding the right balance of individual choice and collective good in making education decisions. *Multiple Choice* is further evidence that Martha is indeed a parent's parent and a teacher's teacher."

> —**Dr. Tony L. Talbert,** Baylor University Fellow, Associate Dean for Strategic Initiatives, Professor, School of Education, Baylor University

"*Multiple Choice* provides thoughtful and practical ways to help parents answer the question, 'How should we educate our child?' This book identifies important things to consider, such as knowing your why and your child's individual needs. It also includes comprehensive information about different schooling options. This information, along with numerous examples and resources, will help parents in the decision-making process."

> —**Dr. Barbara H. Davis,** Professor Emeritus, College of Education, Texas State University

"*Multiple Choice* is a must-read for parents who want the best education for their child. Her warm writing style, unbiased approach, and terrific depth of insight will empower parents to find the best answer for their child's education. *Multiple Choice* has a wealth of confidence-building information and helpful tips in each chapter. I highly recommend this book."

> —**Cheri Fuller,** former Oklahoma Mother of the Year and author of numerous books, including *Raising Motivated Kids*

MULTIPLE
CHOICE

FINDING THE BEST
ANSWER FOR YOUR
CHILD'S EDUCATION

MARTHA SINGLETON

LEAFWOOD
PUBLISHERS
an imprint of Abilene Christian University Press

MULTIPLE CHOICE
Finding the Best Answer for Your Child's Education

LEAFWOOD
P U B L I S H E R S
an imprint of Abilene Christian University Press

Copyright © 2018 by Martha Singleton

ISBN 978-0-89122-473-3

Printed in the United States of America

Published in association with the Hartline Literary Agency, 123 Queenston Drive, Pittsburgh, PA 15235.

Library of Congress Cataloging-in-Publication Data is on file at the Library of Congress, Washington, DC.

Cover design by Bruce Gore | Gore Studio, Inc.
Interior text design by Sandy Armstrong, Strong Designs

Leafwood Publishers is an imprint of Abilene Christian University Press
ACU Box 29138, Abilene, Texas 79699

1-877-816-4455 | www.leafwoodpublishers.com

18 19 20 21 22 23 / 7 6 5 4 3 2 1

*With gratitude to my father,
who always challenged me to think about every
side of an issue, who pushed me to stand on the
courage of my convictions, and who let me know
early that education was a priceless treasure*

*In loving memory of educators who eternally
impacted my life: Elizabeth Hurley, Gladys Batson,
Aubra Nooncaster, and Ann Miller*

Acknowledgments

Thank you to my fantastic agent, Jim Hart, upon whose integrity, effort, and professionalism I can absolutely rely. I also love the music in his Facebook posts.

Thank you to every single person at Leafwood Publishers. The positive attitude, the standard of excellence, and the enthusiasm, encouragement, and support throughout the process made it a joy to work with you.

Thank you to my husband, Greg, whose skill at research took a huge burden off of me. You are always my most effective sounding board, and my favorite partner in every project of life. The prayer and wisdom you brought to our parenting partnership and the creativity you invested in academic adventures for our kids and now our grandkids are at the heart of this book.

Thank you to the education professionals who so graciously granted me their time in interviews and allowed me the benefit of their expertise: Dr. Tony Talbert, Dr. Jake Walters, Ellen Schuknecht, Tim Lambert, and Dr. Michael Korpi.

Thank you to the honest, articulate friends who have allowed me to share their experiences and insight, along with their love and devotion to Christ, in the many examples throughout this book.

Contents

THERE'S MORE THAN ONE RIGHT ANSWER

School was a positive experience for me. Even though I had a couple of teachers along the way who may or may not have been cousins to Harry Potter's cruel teacher, Dolores Umbridge, my parents coached me through it, and I emerged from the process unscathed. Far bigger in my life were my parents, who pushed, punished, and encouraged me as needed, and more than one master teacher who changed my life for the better in various ways.

I played school with the neighborhood kids, and I was always the teacher. I even spent my allowance on a red pencil so that I could grade assignments. I wasn't playing around!

No one was surprised, when it was time for college, that I sought a degree in education. I spent forty-two years in the high school classroom teaching journalism and photography and advising the newspaper, the yearbook, and a daily television news broadcast.

I love kids, and I've seen how education is a part of God's work in developing the abilities and gifts he has placed within

13

each individual to enable them to fulfill God's magnificent purpose for their lives.

I love parents, as well. I was blessed with great ones, I am one, and I want to encourage and cheer on every mom and dad, of whatever age, I meet because while the rewards are so very sweet, the job is extremely hard.

More than anything else we undertake, we want to get our parenting right.

We want our kids to be healthy, happy, well-adjusted children who grow up to be healthy, happy, well-adjusted adults. For Christians, there is the added component of wanting them to find their own vital relationships with Christ and to live fulfilling lives that are meaningful in his kingdom.

From our own experiences in school, whatever those were, we know that what we learn, how we learn, where and from whom we learn, and how we are taught to use that knowledge play a major role in our formation and will affect our confidence and our ability to function every day of our lives.

So figuring out the details of our child's education becomes a huge, almost overwhelming, responsibility and one of the major decisions that we will make as parents.

And there are plenty of loud voices in our culture, putting the hard sell on one venue or the other, pressing parents to the place where fear of making the wrong choice is a bigger motivator than informed, prayerful deliberation.

So, yeah, this is a big deal. But before you start breathing into that paper bag, relax a little bit. I have some good news for you.

This is not a true/false test. It's multiple choice, and the answer, instead of the tricky "none of the above," might just turn out to be "all of the above."

All you need is some educated research, a clear idea of what your child's particular gifts and needs are, and faith that

God *wants* to guide you in making the right choices for each of your kids.

And that's where this book comes in!

The first thing to understand is that there is no one choice that is always right for every child, and no one choice that is always wrong for every child. God creates each of us to be unique and sets us into unique circumstances, always with his best in mind for each of us. So to discover the best choice of school for our children, we must first believe that God cares about each member of our families and that he wants to guide us as we make decisions affecting them. Then, as we gather facts and assess information, we can pray for God to give us wisdom, and then act, secure in the faith that he is guiding us to his best in our specific circumstance.

What we don't want to do is judge, or to let what we perceive as judgment from others influence our decisions.

I can remember feeling uncomfortably shamed by a well-meaning church member when I was expecting our first child. At that time, my husband was on the pastoral staff, and our church was operating a school. I was teaching public school, and while we were each doing what we believed God was asking of us at that time, the income that we had somewhat limited our choices.

This woman, whose husband was a successful surgeon, backed me into a corner to tell me that God expected me to stay at home with my children and, when the time came, to teach them at home. I can remember thinking, *Sister, if you think that, then maybe you should increase your giving so that the church can increase what we pay youth pastors!* That conversation, and my reaction to it, made me feel really terrible for a while, until I was able to pray about it. I realized that if my husband and I were faithfully following what we were certain was God's leading for us, then we could count on his protection, provision, and blessing for our children in those circumstances, too.

Over the years, I have watched friends homeschool their children, some with great success, some with mediocrity, and some whose outcomes could only be labeled "major fail."

I have been closely associated with private schools that were worth every extra penny parents paid in tuition, and I have known others that were woefully insufficient.

I have seen parents' worst nightmares come true for their children in public schools, and I have seen others whose children thrived there.

And I have seen a variety of outcomes for different siblings within the same family.

The one thing I am certain of is that wherever you may choose to educate your child, the most crucial component is *you*. Ultimately, not only your decision, but your day-to-day participation will be the major factor in your child's education and preparation for life as an adult.

This book is designed to assist you in several ways.

After guiding you in identifying your goals for your children's education, we will discover how to assess your kids' gifts and abilities and how they each learn best.

Armed with that information, we will take an objective look at the strengths and weaknesses of each form of schooling, hearing from parents, teachers, and students who have experienced them.

I have included sections within the chapters to give you additional context and resources to help in your decision-making. Study the Example sections include interviews and stories of families whose experiences in educating their children can give you extra insight. Do Your Homework sections give you ideas and encouragement for your role at home in guiding and enriching your child's learning, no matter which educational venue you choose. And the Pop Quiz sections at the end of chapters will give you questions to help direct you as you think and continue the decision-making process. Outside Reading sections are lists of resources that will give you more details on the subjects covered in the chapter. And the occasional Extra Credit sections will give you some practical "hacks" that can help you as you work with your children. To save you time and a lot of tedious effort, all the links are available on our website, www.kitchentablecurriculum.com.

Through it all, we will examine ways that parents will need to guide, support, and enrich their kids' spiritual, intellectual, social, and emotional growth along their educational journeys, for each of the venues they might choose.

In the end, you will find yourself with the facts and understanding you need to sort through your questions and seek God with the confidence of both faith and understanding, so that you can trust your decision on behalf of your child.

And hopefully, you will have picked up some exciting and creative ways to make learning a joy for your whole family.

Section One
MATCHING

It is a source of humor in my family now to look back on photos of Christmas dinner at my grandmother's house, where all three of her sons-in-law are fulfilling the duty of wearing the shirts she had given them on Christmas Eve: exactly alike, year after year after year. But imagine what would happen at your house if, on Christmas morning, your two-year-old daughter, your five-year-old son, and your ten-year-old daughter each received exactly the same American Girl doll and book from Santa.

In this section, we'll explore ways to match your particular family's goals and each individual child's needs in order to help you come up with a personalized "shopping list" for the best educational fit for each child.

Chapter One

KNOW YOUR WHY

I attended Baylor University during the period that sports historians call the bleakest in all of the Bears' years of fielding a football team, which goes back to 1899. So it makes sense that I would be a huge fan of Robert Griffin III, the quarterback and Heisman Trophy winner who led the recent era of success that Baylor enjoyed. (Gotta say it here: Sic'em, Bears!)

But I also admire "RGIII" for his character and integrity off the field, and I respect, along with his penchant for superhero-themed socks, the wisdom that he shares about life in general.

One of his catchphrases as a team leader applies in our search for the right place to educate our kids—"know your why." Before we begin our task, we need to have our "why" clearly in mind for three different things.

Why Do We Educate Our Kids?
There is an obvious answer to that question. We want them to have the basic knowledge and skills necessary to function in life. Beyond that, we want them to be fully prepared to provide for themselves and their families, whether that means learning skills

for a trade or gaining higher education and certification needed to practice a profession.

But for Christ-followers, the "why" has much deeper, more significant implications.

The Broadway musical hit *Big River* opens with Huck Finn complaining that school is a waste of time that would be better spent fishing. In the first big number, the whole town sings to Huck that he has to learn to read so that he can read the Bible, and thus avoid going to hell. While this is a somewhat funny song, it also gets to what is perhaps the bedrock of why we educate our children, the reason that for centuries Jewish children, including Jesus, have been sent to Hebrew school. A broad education, which exposes our children to facts about the universe in which we live, actually is a study of God and his ways. A study of mathematics and science reveals to us the complete and precise order, from the vast to the most intricate detail, of his creation.

I struggled with math throughout my entire education, from first grade through college trigonometry, which was required then for a degree in secondary education. (Imagine my jealousy when I discovered, thirty years later, that my son was only required to take a course called "Ideas in Math" for the same degree. I'm *still* not over it!) I hated every minute of math classes.

But after I was out of school and had become a teacher myself, someone pointed out that the digits of multiples of nine always add up to nine! And the correct number always starts one numeral less than the multiplier! (So, if you were never clued in on this, here are a couple of examples. First, $9 \times 2 = 18$. The sum of $1 + 8$ is 9, and the 1 that starts the 18 is one numeral less than the multiplier, 2. In the same way, $9 \times 3 = 27$. The correct answer will start with 2 and then 7, as the other number would add up to 9, so 9×3 is 27.) Amazing! Wonder-filled!

Numbers are what they are. Mathematical facts never change. Two plus two will *always* equal four, and will *never* total either five or three. This is similar to God in that he too does not change. He introduces himself to Moses as "I AM who I AM" (Exod. 3:14 NLT). God is the same yesterday, today, and forever. Today, numbers fascinate me and speak to me of a creator and of designed order in the universe.

Sometime when you have about fifteen minutes, gather your kids around the computer and search for the video of Louie Giglio speaking about the sounds of stars, pulsars, and whales.[1] Talk about the wonders of studying science! Of course we want our children to know all there is about this place where we live, and the one who created it for us.

The study of social sciences, from history to economics to psychology, gives us a sense of how God has made humans, how we interact with one another, and how he interacts with us over centuries of life on Earth.

In English courses and the study of foreign languages, we learn to communicate effectively, both orally and in writing, and to develop the skill that distinguishes us from all other species.

And in the fine and performing arts, our children learn to nurture and express their souls, enabling them to discover and express compassion, hope, and the creativity that is a part of God's making us in his image.

Knowing and understanding truth, as it can be found in the classroom and laboratory and studio, is an important part of knowing and understanding the One who said, "I am the way, the truth, and the life" (John 14:6 NLT).

Why Is My Child's Education Important?

As Christians, we believe that God has a specific purpose and a magnificent plan for the life of each child he has entrusted to us to parent, and education is the first step toward preparing them to be the adults he created them to be and enabling them to fulfill that unique calling for their lives.

In addition to the basic knowledge and skills to be gained in the basic subjects of English/language arts, social studies, math, science, and computer competency, our children need to learn from participating in extracurricular activities or athletics. Through such experiences, they develop crucial social skills, discipline, self-discipline, and the ability to solve problems, organize, and work with other people.

The sum total of your child's educational experience will be of major influence on how, as an adult, he sees himself in relation to the world, and will be the foundation of confidence from which she will navigate life.

So it is of great importance to choose where and how each child will be educated, and to give the best of ourselves to ensuring that the education they receive equips them to be the adults God wants them to be.

Why Will This Decision Be Important for My Family in General?

Where, when, and how your child will be educated affects a broad area of the day-to-day life of your entire family, in addition to the outcomes in your child's life. The time you spend, whether it is in driving to and from school and activities or in teaching at home, overseeing homework, or enriching instruction, will influence how your days, weeks, and weekends look.

Social contacts, not only for the child but for you as parents will be greatly influenced by your choice of schooling.

Finances will be a major consideration in making your choice, as well.

All these things must be considered together, and carefully prayed over, so that you can approach your decision-making with wise, God-directed purpose.

POP QUIZ

1. List three main goals you have as a parent for the outcome of your child's K–12 education overall.

2. Why is each important to you?

OUTSIDE READING

Louie Giglio, pastor of Passion City Church in Atlanta and founder of the Passion Movement, shared awesome thoughts about God, his creation, and who he is in the talk called "Stars and Whales Mash-up," which can be found online. It gives us the real reason we want to learn more.

In the interest of "knowing your why," here's a great description of what we want our kids to be, courtesy of Veritas Academy in Austin, Texas:

www.veritasacademy.net/mission-and-values/

Chapter Two

KNOW YOUR CHILD

If you are the parent to more than one child, this is no big news flash—every single kid is different. I mean *really* different.

Temperament, personality, likes and dislikes, sleeping pattern, food preferences, scratch back or sing to sleep, Dora or Doc McStuffins, time-out or lost privileges.

Just ask my daughter and son-in-law, who accidentally but gratefully discovered that the only thing that would stop their youngest son's incessant, near-hysterical crying as an infant was to play "You Were Always on My Mind" by Willie Nelson. The effect was instant and unfailing. Pretty big deal for people who feature Toby Mac and Broadway show tunes on their playlists.

We learn early to know which cry is for hunger, which one means "I'm sleepy but I can't give up," and which one means to run because something hurts. We know their favorite pajamas, favorite snacks, and favorite toys.

When it comes to guiding their educations, we also must set ourselves the task of knowing how each child can best learn and then applying this knowledge to determine how they will be taught.

A part of earning a degree in education includes developing the skills to understand and identify each student's learning style, which is simply the most effective way they learn.

For example, a student who is what we call a tactile, or kinesthetic learner, may have a hard time sitting still and listening to a story, but would delight in using paper dolls to act it out, or in memorizing facts by reciting in rhythm and clapping or dancing. A tactile learner will develop writing skills by arranging words on slips of paper to form a sentence, or learn geography by working a puzzle map.

Or maybe your child needs to see pictures or charts and be able to visualize what she is learning about. Visual learners will want to be close to the front with an unobstructed view. When doing research online, an older child will want to click "images" or go to YouTube before looking at written research. Visual learners will want to watch the movie *before* they read the book.

Auditory learners like lectures, love discussions, and gather clues from the speaker's inflection and tone of voice. If this is your child's style, you will notice that he will want to have information read aloud to him. An auditory learner will also benefit from talking through information before he reads it.

Excellent educators attempt to address each student's learning style over the scope of a unit of study. While not every lesson or activity will target every child's style, a school or a classroom that does not attempt to create opportunities for the variety of styles will not have maximum effectiveness. A major reason that straight online instruction is not more widely used is that it gives no opportunity for students to approach material and skills through their own most effective learning style. As a parent, knowing each child's strongest learning style will be valuable as you assess which learning environment will be most effective for your child.

Similarly, Harvard education professor Howard Gardner's concept of what he calls "multiple intelligences," or ways to demonstrate intellectual ability, would be helpful for parents to identify, particularly because I think of them as being related to specific God-given gifts and callings that we might want to focus on helping our child develop. There is some overlap with learning styles, but Gardner's list is varied and a bit more detailed. It is also possible for a child to have more than one "intelligence."

For instance, Gardner identifies "verbal/linguistic intelligence" as the ability to use words. These people think in words instead of pictures and are good at both written and spoken communication. According to him, their skills would include things like storytelling, explaining, teaching, or convincing someone of their point of view. Knowing that this kind of person might find a career as a poet, journalist, teacher, lawyer, or politician, parents would want to be sure that their child was reading widely, and to encourage creative writing or participation in student publications or speech and debate at school.

Other intelligences include things like musical/rhythmic intelligence, interpersonal intelligence (being able to relate to and understand others), and logical/mathematical intelligence. To explore all nine areas in detail, read the Do Your Homework: Multiple Intelligences section on page 31.

It is easy for us as parents to just assume that our child's learning style, abilities, and interests will naturally reflect our own. Athletic parents will include plenty of physical activity in their kids' lives, while others might focus on a reading hour and multiple trips to the library. Parents who love music will provide instruments and lessons, and so on. This is natural, and exposure to a variety of activities and interests is always a positive thing. However, we need to be alert to the possibility that our children may not be exactly like us.

I remember hiding in the bathroom to read a book as a middle school student, knowing that if my mom saw me reading, she would say something like, "If you're not doing anything, why don't you take your sister for a walk or take out the trash." I always wanted to say, "I *am* doing something—I'm *reading*," but even at twelve years old, I knew that would not be wise!

As I got older, my parents were extremely supportive of my writing endeavors, and they made certain that I had the extra time and transportation to participate in my high school journalism program. However, because she was more interpersonal and kinetic in her approach to things, my mom just didn't get the idea that, for me, reading was much more than a boredom buster.

I am reminded of a former student whose parents were both highly successful in careers in business and law, and who naturally had high expectations for their daughter. She worked hard and did well in her classwork, but she was not going to be valedictorian, and she struggled with the fear that she was disappointing them.

Then she became a photographer for the yearbook staff and fell in love with photographing people. She was extremely talented and had what I called a "natural eye" for composition and for knowing "the moment" to trip the shutter.

Today, three decades later, she is a renowned portrait photographer whose award-winning work is featured in international shows and publications. She has traveled the world photographing weddings and is in demand to do portraits of celebrities and their families. Of course, her parents, whose true concern was only that she would be able to find fulfillment and be able to support herself, are wildly proud of her.

It is important for parents to study each child and become aware of the various interests, talents, abilities, and approaches to life and learning that characterize each. Being armed with knowledge of your child's learning style and intelligences will be invaluable as you seek out the best method of educating each of your children, and fulfill your duty of preparing them for fulfilling, meaningful lives as adults.

DO YOUR HOMEWORK:
Multiple Intelligences

In developmental psychologist Howard Gardner's book *Frames of Mind: The Theory of Multiple Intelligences*, he developed his theory that there is no true way to measure intelligence, but that the brain contains a broad range of abilities with which to learn and understand.[1]

He explains that the old way of measuring intelligence really only measured logical and mathematical intelligence.

His theory is that limiting the scope and definition of intelligence keeps us from fully understanding how the brain works, and when it comes to educating our children, this would be a crucial mistake.

We all know adults who are amazing musicians or accomplished designers or artists, but who struggled with math in school. According to Gardner, these students were no less intelligent than those succeeding at multiplication, or even calculus, but simply operated in different intelligence areas.

As parents interested in providing the most effective education for our children, it is worth understanding the nine areas that Gardner explains in his book: the variety of areas and approaches that are part of each child.

Waterfalls, Caterpillars, and Organic Gardeners

You know that friend who turns pale and nearly jumps onto the couch in dismay when your pet enters the room? Or the one, like me, who kills every plant within a three-block radius just by breathing? People without a strong sense of nature.

On the other hand, think about the one who gets down on the floor and plays with your pet, or the one, like my son-in-law, who can make every plant flourish, who can identify various plants and breeds of animals, who instinctively knows exactly where to cast to catch a fish, who possesses an intrinsic sense of how the earth works and how to make it work for him.

Back when making a living for families relied on agricultural or hunting skills, this was a crucial ability to have. Today, people with a strong naturalistic understanding might seek jobs in botany, agronomy, or even as entrepreneurs in this day of farm-to-table markets and restaurants.

I believe our grandson has a strong naturalistic instinct, as he devours the "Grumpy Gardener" column in his mom's copies of *Southern Living*. We allowed him to select a variety of cactus plants for our rock garden and have been amazed at the beauty—and health—of the spot he designed. And he's only eight years old!

Beethoven, Beatles, or Bieber

I can remember pounding away at the drudgery of piano practice, with one eye always on the timer, for the year of piano lessons that my parents offered me, with no appreciable results. (The same letdown came of the ballet lessons and private art lessons they tried for me as well, bless their hearts. But finally an English teacher told me I was a good writer! At last, my talent was defined!)

But if your child is attracted to sounds and seems to be constantly drumming a rhythm, singing, or otherwise trying to make music, musical intelligence might be one of his strong leanings.

If your youngster drops her Duplos to go stand by the TV when music comes on, then you might want to make it a point to give her access to toy instruments and consider including music lessons of some sort in her education.

Long before Gardner came up with his list, the ABC song and the musical list of books of the Bible were helping kids learn by appealing to their musical instincts. The ability to deeply appreciate or create music has been linked in studies to those who also excel at mathematics and to those who are able to express emotion easily.

Whether an individual grows up to pursue a career in music or not, those with "musical intelligence" will be able to use that to maintain their mental and emotional health.

Easy as 1-2-3

While the phrase "fun with numbers" might seem like an oxymoron to many of us, there are people who find delight in logic puzzles, strategy games, and even in solving the dreaded twenty arithmetic problems the teacher assigned for homework. They are adept at winning arguments with their logical reasoning skills and ability to think abstractly. This child will not be highly motivated by simply memorizing answers for a multiple choice test, but will find satisfaction in the process of recognizing patterns and relationships, and figuring out the why and how for herself. In addition to being mathematicians or physicists, children with a strong logical-mathematical intelligence might gravitate to a career involving a form of research or detective work.

Cookies, Milk, and the Reason for Suffering in the World Today

When our children come up with questions or observations about the meaning of life and our role in the universe that give us pause and make us want to exclaim, "Whoa, that's deep," it could signify a strong existential intelligence. These children will ponder why they were born, what happens when people die, and other philosophical questions. While there is less research and commentary about this particular trait, it has also been referred to as spiritual or moral intelligence and might produce a leaning toward writing or ministry with a philosophical basis.

Can't We All Just Get Along?

Remember the kid you knew in school that everyone liked? She could walk up to any group gathered in the cafeteria—the jocks, the techies, the hipsters, the bro's, or the anime club members—and have them talking and laughing in no time.

If your child demonstrates the ability to sense the moods of people, to consider others' ideas and points of view, and to connect, with either words or just a smile, then you are looking at a strong interpersonal intelligence. This innate ability to interact with others often manifests itself in leadership roles among students. Adults with this strength often become politicians, teachers, social workers, or actors, according to studies.

Basketball, Ballet, Whip, or Nae Nae

The opposite of a klutz, a person with kinesthetic intelligence is able to stay coordinated and move their body or objects with grace and skill. A good sense of timing and things like good eye-hand coordination give them success in dancing, playing sports, or manipulating objects.

If your child easily catches a ball, loves and excels at tumbling or ballet class, or can construct intricate, amazing Lego creations, then this would be a strong intelligence.

In addition to the obvious professional athlete or dancer, this mind-body connection also shows up in surgeons and craftspeople.

Use Your Words

This is what sets humans apart from animals. The increasing ability to think in words and make others understand us is entertaining to watch as our babies say their first words, and progress from stringing one or two words together to speaking in sentences to describing their first day at kindergarten.

While all people use this intelligence, some, like bloggers, novelists, poets, playwrights, journalists, and public speakers, are more strongly motivated and skilled in the use of written and spoken language than others.

In children, linguistic intelligence shows up in a child's enjoyment of word puzzles, reading, storytelling, and writing. "Word-smart" kids will like encountering new words and will stretch to include them in their vocabulary.

We still laugh at the memory of our son, at about three years old, talking about wearing his first shirt, tie, and pants to church on Easter Sunday. After proudly trying on his new clothes, he announced, "I am going to be cas-u-al!" What he missed in meaning, he made up for in effort to communicate. Today, by the way, he is a high school journalism teacher.

"What I Am Is Who I Am"

Will.i.am sang about it on *Sesame Street*. It's a strong, healthy sense of who we are and what we are to be and do in our world that comes naturally in a child early.

For most people, the adolescent years present a somewhat unpleasant period of self-doubt and insecurity, made even more challenging by the need to be making choices and decisions that affect the rest of our lives. At a time when we struggle with self-awareness and self-acceptance, many are also having to choose a career or vocation, decide where and how to train for that, and even trying to select a mate.

However, the teen with a strong intrapersonal intelligence has the ability to understand and accept himself and to put his thoughts and emotions into a healthy context, along with an understanding of life and human nature in general. This self-awareness allows him to wisely plan his life and his role in the world.

A teen with this strength, while self-motivated, may also be a bit shy.

In my role as a high school journalism teacher, I made it a practice to ask each of my students often, "What do you want to do after you graduate?" Most of them over the years would look at me like deer in the headlights and mumble, "Uh, I don't know," at which point I would begin a running conversation to guide them into thinking about their passions, their gifts, their strengths, their goals, and what careers might allow them to use that.

But every year, I would find two or three who had immediate answers for my questions, and a road map for how they would achieve their goals. These were the ones who had a strong natural intrapersonal intelligence. And interestingly, they were often the same ones who avoided a lot of angst and drama in their dating relationships, as well.

Cubes and Cones and Spheres

If you have one kid who can look at the "You are here" map at a theme park and guide the whole family to the nearest pizza restaurant, that's the one who has a grip on relationships among objects. The innate ability to understand things in three dimensions is what Gardner calls spatial intelligence.

A few weeks ago, a dear friend of our daughter who is now a world-renowned opera star presented a benefit concert on a local university campus. Our daughter was taking a busload of her drama students straight from school to hear him, so we picked up our grandson and planned to meet her there.

The campus has grown exponentially in the past few years, so we were unsure of the best place to park in relation to the location of the new concert hall. After my husband drove as far as GPS would take us, I tried to get us the rest of the way using a small copy of a campus map. I wasn't having much luck reading the small print, even with my glasses on, and Greg was circling and backtracking, all to the kind of lively discussion that might occur in such circumstances between two people who have been married almost four decades.

Evidently, Josiah, riding in the back seat, deduced that his G's were completely lost and that this emergency was going to require his stepping in.

We parked, and before we could even exit the lot, Josiah started asking people we encountered, "Sir, can you tell me the way to the fine arts concert hall?"

We were stunned at his take-charge attitude, and even more surprised when he took the lead, correctly directing our path across green spaces and around buildings to our destination. The icing on the cake was when we topped a small hill, and he told us, "As I suspected, that is the concert hall over there."

As we suspected, he has a pretty good spatial intelligence. And we really *may* need him in our old age.

Highly creative, these people have strong imaginations, are good at manipulating images, and have artistic or graphic skills. They could end up as architects, sculptors, or pilots.

Children with this strength will love to solve jigsaw puzzles or mazes, and may spend lots of time daydreaming or doodling. Building a dollhouse or laying out a town in the sandbox with roads and a highway system will consume them for an entire day. Studying maps and the globe, or looking at Google Earth and zooming in and out would be engaging to them.

As you go through this list, you will probably find more than one description that applies to each of your children. But there will be a few that really stand out, and these are the ones that are dominant in your child. This understanding will be extremely useful as you set out to help your kids gain an effective education that allows them to develop into capable, fulfilled, contributing adults.

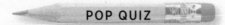

POP QUIZ

1. As I consider each child, what strikes me as their favorite activity? What might that indicate about how they think and will best learn?

2. How does my child like to use free time?

3. How does my child approach/interact with other people?

4. What sort of learning environment does it seem to me will be most effective for my child?

OUTSIDE READING

If your learning style and intelligences are demanding something more scholarly, you can check out these online resources. But if you're feeling pretty bold and confident at this point, you can skip this part completely and proceed to the next section. However, this link also contains a sample assessment to identify intelligences, in case you want to look at just that.

www.literacynet.org/mi/assessment/findyourstrengths.html

For a more detailed look at learning styles, kidspot.com has checklists that will lead you to some more depth in discovering your child's learning style. At the end of the kidspot webpost, you'll find a link that will take you further into learning styles.

www.kidspot.com.au/school/primary/learning
-and-behaviour/learning-styles-in-children

Here's another in-depth survey to help you assess your child's (or your own) learning style.

www.ldpride.net/learningstyles.mi.htm

Knowing and understanding learning styles and multiple intelligences is vital in accentuating your child's education experience. The more you can learn about it, the better off you and your child are. Here's another great resource for assessment.

www.literacynet.org/mi/assessment/cgi-bin/results.cgi

Reminder: you can find all of the links in this book at *www.kitchen tablecurriculum.com.*

Section Two
MULTIPLE CHOICE

It's always great to have inside information from people who know. Whether it's finding the great pizzeria just a block away where the locals get their slice of pie while all the other tourists are crowding into the McDonald's on Times Square, or learning that there's free parking at the Museum of Texas History in downtown Austin that you could use on a UT football game day while everyone else is paying big bucks to walk a lot farther to the stadium, there are some things that we just don't figure out unless we're lucky enough to get a tip from the right people.

   I remember a ski trip I took early in my (brief) career as a snow skier. I had taken enough lessons to be able to make my way down the slope in one piece, but as a twenty-two-year-old college gradu-ate working at my first job in my profession, it was

really humiliating that I fell getting off the lift . . . Every. Single. Time. All morning long, everyone from advanced skiers to toddlers heading for the bunny slope had to swerve to avoid me as they came off the lift.

Finally, right after lunch, I happened to ride up on a seat with a bright and friendly ten-year-old boy who had spent the morning whipping around me more than once as I struggled to get up and get out of the way of others exiting the lift.

"Y'know," he told me with a grin as we neared the top, "you wouldn't be falling if you stopped trying to stand up when you get off."

"What? What do you mean?" I asked.

"Just put your skis down and lean forward, and let the lift seat push you. It's easy," he instructed.

Astonished to find that there was a technique, and somewhat miffed that none of my instructors or ski buddies had filled me in on that little detail, I followed his directions and sailed smoothly off the lift and onto the trail, just like everyone else.

Before you start your task of selecting the best mode of education for your child, there's some insider information that could keep you from crashing before you get started. So climb on the lift; you're about to take a ride with an expert!

Dr. Tony Talbert is a highly respected professor in the School of Education at Baylor University, and his work overseeing students as they gain experience teaching in area public schools and academies gives him rare insight into the working of education as it is happening today.

He sat down with me one morning at a coffee shop just off campus to share his observations and conclusions and offer insight to parents.

Whether they will be choosing a public school, a Christian school, or teaching their children themselves at home, there is an approach to the desired outcomes that parents should consider to start with.

"Parents must decide if they are committed simply to an information-based system, which focuses on factual and conceptual knowledge, or a transformation-based system, which is procedural and metacognitive," Talbert said.

Metacognition refers to higher-order thinking that allows for understanding and analysis, especially in the learning process. It includes knowledge about when and how to use specific strategies for learning and problem solving.

In a time when facts are instantly available via an online search, the list of skills necessary for success is shifting in a way that would make transformation-based education more applicable.

"The role in the twenty-first century of the Four C's—critical thinking, creative action, communicative collaboration, and contemplative reflection—must not be rejected by Christian parents and guardians," Talbert said. "If the Christian philosophy has relevance, it must be able to co-exist within a pluralistic world.

"I'm often struck by how many pro-capitalist Christians call for free market practices, yet reject the same within their own and their children's exposure to diverse ideas within education," he said. "If Christianity is 'big T truth,' then it must expose itself consistently to an environment where 'wondering' and 'inquisitiveness' are the centerpiece of the education system."

Talbert sees an overarching approach to education that wise parents should seek in whatever venue they consider.

"I embrace the notion of James Paul Gee that calls for synchronized intelligence as a way of organizing people and their digital tools to solve problems, produce knowledge, and allow people to count and contribute," he said. "This is truly an equitable and inclusive system of education that allows educators to use metacognitive curriculum to teach procedural, conceptual, and then factual knowledge.

"We must envision education for the twenty-first century where we may not know the component parts of 'knowledge' that will exist in 2029, but we have prepared students to inquire, explore, analyze, synthesize, evaluate, create, problem solve, and critically ponder, regardless of what passes as 'official' curriculum," he said.

Talbert offers parents who are seeking the transformative method of education for their children a list of key questions to ask as they research and compare their choices of schools, or as they select and prepare curriculum for teaching their kids at home:

- Is the school/curriculum teaching students *how* to think, rather than *what* to think?
- Is the focus on how to problem *solve*, rather than how to problem *avoid*?
- Is the education system providing opportunities for experiences that allow the student to be exposed to factual, conceptual, procedural, and metacognitive knowledge and understanding?
- Does the system provide the student with a diverse array of learning experiences, environments, and encounters among the full spectrum of student peers that make up our social institutions and cultural conversations?
- Are the learning and teaching environments and curriculum intentionally inclusive and differentiated (tailored to the specific needs of the particular group or individuals within a group)?
- Is your desire for your student to be engaged in the society and culture in a way that allows for transformation of self and others?

Armed with your own thoughtful, prayerful answers to the questions and choices posed by Dr. Talbert, you now have that "insider's edge" that will help you more successfully navigate the possibilities you are about to explore.

Chapter Three

HOMESCHOOL

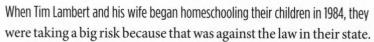

When Tim Lambert and his wife began homeschooling their children in 1984, they were taking a big risk because that was against the law in their state.

"We had a hard time finding curriculum," he told me in our phone conversation, "because providers didn't want to sell to us."[1]

Today, homeschooling is legal in all states, with more than two million students in the United States being homeschooled.

"These days, the curriculum challenge is in narrowing it down from the many choices available," said Lambert, who is president of the Texas Home School Coalition Association.

Then, as now, the number one motivation for parents to homeschool their children is a character issue. Many parents whose first priority is to disciple their kids and pass on their own faith believe that using the time at home is the best way to do that.

"Increasingly, in public education and even in private schools, the curriculum, the environment, and even the friends their kids make are becoming more and more negative, and parents are finding they just can't take that," Lambert said.

There are other reasons that parents decide to homeschool, in addition to that overarching desire to focus on spiritual training.

"You can customize their education to meet your child's specific needs," Lambert said. "By using the tutorial method, parents can even allow their student to become a child actor, for instance, or to pursue becoming an Olympic athlete. It is an efficient way to educate children while allowing them to pursue their interests full-time.

"And some parents just look at the situation and say, 'I can do a better job,'" he said. "They are smart, and they have the ability to provide a wide variety of experiences, not bound by an eight-hour school day."

Homeschooling may be the answer for families who live in unsafe situations, too.

"For a family living in the inner city, it can be the way to provide physical protection for their children," Lambert said. "Parents can be creative with the schedule. We know of single parents who homeschool after they get home from work. There is nothing that says it has to take place during the traditional school day."

It is important, as parents work through the decision-making process, to remain focused on your family's "why" for education. If you find yourself drawn to the idea of avoiding the pressure of getting everyone up, dressed, fed, and out the door on time, with plenty of field trips to the mall, these might not be the best reasons to homeschool.

As negative and unsettling as parts of today's culture can be, an irrational fear of contact with anyone outside of our tight family and church circles would not be the healthiest motivation, either, if the goal is to raise children who can successfully navigate life and handle adversity. Only parents themselves can evaluate their thoughts and feelings in that area, but it is important to be certain that there is balance in the approach to the choice they will make.

It is also crucial to keep in mind the basic goal for education. We want to give our children the knowledge, skills, and tools they will need to understand the world and God's working in it, and to achieve any task that God may have for them in their lives, which means that a huge burden of responsibility falls upon the shoulders of parents who homeschool.

I will always remember a conversation I had with a young man in the high school Sunday school class I taught, who was coming to the end of his final year of homeschooling. I made a reference to a character in the literary classic *To Kill a Mockingbird*, and he had no idea what I was talking about.

Surprised, I began to ask him about the literary works he had read and which ones he had particularly enjoyed. I was shocked to find that he had not read even one great work. No Shakespeare, no Robert Frost, no Tolkien, no C. S. Lewis—not even one of the Chronicles of Narnia. He had read a couple of books from the Babysitter's Club series, but that was it—not even a book from the extensive list of purely entertaining Christian young adult fiction.

I think my facial expression must have shown my surprise and dismay because he told me, "It doesn't matter. I'm just going to run my dad's store." Interestingly, he ended up years later assisting in a global ministry and had to overcome some major hurdles to achieve the training required.

That is certainly not the case for most homeschool students, but it should serve as a sort of cautionary tale as parents examine their goals and purpose for educating their children.

Lambert noted that according to research by Dr. Brian Ray of the National Home Education Research Institute, while in traditional schools the parents' education and income level can often be predictors of their children's success, the same is not true of homeschool students.

"Parents often educate themselves in the process of teaching their own children," Lambert explained. "There's a high level of commitment on the part of parents who love their kids enough to do the hard things."

He says there are two extreme ends of the spectrum when it comes to how individual parents will approach the job of homeschooling.

"On one end, there's the very organized, regimented parent, and on the other, there's what I call the 'unschooler,' who lacks any organization. The right place is really in the middle. The most effective parents give direction and help their youngsters learn the basics, but they also use flexibility in seeing to it that their kids gain experiences and develop maturity.

"We tend to think of it all from the perspective of our own experience, but that's not always the most effective approach. There are online classes, and some are even dual credit courses that can count toward the college degree. There are so many opportunities for hands-on learning and field trips, too. Be open-minded," he said.

Parents who choose to homeschool should begin from the legal perspective, according to Lambert.

"Research the laws in your state," he said. "The law varies from state to state, even for things like how to withdraw your student from public school and how to register as homeschoolers. Knowing the legal requirements is an important reason for parents to get connected with homeschool organizations at both the local and state levels because the laws can change."

As far as the actual home instruction goes, Lambert's first advice is for the parent to relax and find the right rhythm for their youngsters.

"Use the resources as a starting point," he said, "but just focus on the basics. With the kindergarteners and early elementary grades, you can take it slowly. Read to them a lot, and teach them to read.

"Sometimes the moms are overwhelmed and even fearful that they won't be adequate for the job. We recommend that parents give their kids the standardized achievement tests, not for the children, but for the parent to be able to measure progress. The test results often shock parents when they see that their kids really are learning," Lambert said.

As the kids grow past the elementary level, it becomes time to set and pursue long-term goals. Lambert thinks that beginning middle school is the right time to start the process of getting children ready for college.

"Begin by thinking about what your child wants to study, and assessing colleges where those majors are offered," he said. "Look at what each of those individual institutions require for acceptance, and be sure to work those things into the curriculum and experiences you are providing.

"It's a multi-year process. You don't want to get to the last year and discover your child doesn't meet all the requirements for admission to the college he wants to attend. By ninth grade, the student should have a feel for what they want in both academics and the whole college experience. If you know that early enough, you can frame studies to include what they need, and the admission process will be much easier, and your child's horizons will be expanded," he said.

As you give prayerful consideration to what will be best for your child and your family, it will be wise to keep two important things in mind. Because of the resources and support widely available, there is no need to be so intimidated by the task that you automatically dismiss it. But at the same time, the responsibility of educating your children is a serious one that will require a major commitment of time, thought, and energy on a daily basis.

Lambert has one last word of encouragement for parents engaged in the decision-making process.

"Be open-minded. You have the freedom to do whatever you choose, and your decision can even change from year to year as you do what seems best for your family," he said.

Study the Example: *Sarah*

For the whole of Sarah's education, she was taught at home by her mom. Today, as the mother of four school-age children and a toddler, Sarah continues that pattern by teaching her own kids at home.

"It was good for me because my mother was able to teach to the specific way that I learned. I gained many strengths from being homeschooled," she said. "In my experience, I was able to get a very well-rounded education. Not only did I get an education that fit my learning style, but my parents also made sure that we learned things like hard work. From a young age, we would get to go to work with my dad," Sarah said. "I learned about things like building and painting, and as I got older, I learned to balance his books, record receipts, and work on taxes. I also had many, many opportunities to spend time with my grandparents, where I got to learn things like gardening and canning. I think that this type of education, which included book smarts as well as street smarts, is very important," she said.

Looking back on her own experience, Sarah can see only one drawback, which she characterizes as temporary.

"At times as a teenager I had a feeling of missing out on some things that go on at schools, like parties and football games. I sometimes wished I could have played sports at the school, but we did have a prom to go to," she said.

When the time came to make decisions for her own children's schooling, Sarah and her husband were very clear on their reasons for choosing to homeschool.

"First and foremost, this is what God has for our family at this time," she said.

"Another reason we chose this was because of my husband's career. As a firefighter, his hours are not like most. We like the idea of homeschooling because on his days at home, he is able to be involved in their education. If our kids were attending a school, there would be very little time to spend with him. Another reason we chose homeschooling is the fact that we can teach them according to the way their brains work. I like that I can very specifically create a learning environment and curriculum that best suits each child."

Tailoring the day to meet each child's specific needs is her ongoing challenge.

"A typical school day would be me making up a daily to-do list for my fifth graders. They work independently for the most part," Sarah said. "I then have the second and third grader sitting at the table with their books. I spend my time working back and forth with them. I am available to help the older two as they need. We will usually complete most subjects by lunch time, but will usually do reading together after lunch.

"Keeping my momentum is the biggest challenge as the kids get older because the situation changes from year to year. Right now, I also have a toddler, and for instance, if one of the kids isn't fitting with the books that I have and I need to adjust what I'm doing, then trying to do that and still give my very best to each one requires a lot," she said.

"The benefits to our family have been numerous, such as the time we have together, and the ability to travel where we could not have otherwise with traditional school schedules," Sarah said.

"There are a few of our kiddos that have been ready to start school early, so they are ahead, gradewise. We have really been able to watch and enjoy the different learning styles of each child."

"My second grader just thinks differently from the others, for example," Sarah said. "She's a lefty, and she's very artistic, and needs to know why on everything. She really threw me when she was learning to read because she and I don't think alike.

"I was determined to teach her to read phonetically, but she didn't like it that the word 'the' was not phonetic. She insisted that it should be pronounced 't-he' so she just boycotted it, and skipped it whenever she came to it in a sentence. I had to be creative, and it took a while before she accepted it as a sight word," Sarah laughed.

Often parents wonder if they would be effective teaching their children at home. "Anybody can," Sarah said, "but not everybody should.

"It takes patience, the ability to adapt to different learning styles, flexibility, and the willingness to learn along with your child," she said. "It's a big sacrifice, and you have to be willing to give all of yourself. You have to be open-minded and not set on just one way of learning or teaching, or on relying on just one curriculum.

"If the parent is strictly doing it for convenience, if they don't have the time to dedicate to teaching, or they're unable to provide consistency in teaching, it's probably not for you. I knew a mom who did it just because she didn't want to have to get up early to get her kids ready for school every day, and that was a disaster," Sarah said. "Either way, you have to pay attention to how your kids are responding, and be willing to accept that it's not for you, before it begins to negatively affect the education of your kids."

Along with the significant investment of time, parents who homeschool need to be prepared to invest finances, too.

"You could keep it fairly inexpensive, especially in the younger years," Sarah said, "but it will cost more the older the child gets. You might also choose to have your child tutored in any or all subjects, and that adds up. In the upper grades, the books are more expensive, and there is a wider range of activities for them to participate in. You have to pay for belonging to a co-op or for them to attend a science lab or tutoring."

With their "why" for homeschooling their children firmly in place, Sarah and her husband have clear goals that measure their success in educating each child.

"As a Christian, I would define a successful homeschool education as teaching my kids to understand and recognize who and what God created them to be. I hope that they walk away from this knowing how to live in the world, and how to continue to learn throughout life. I hope they have good study skills. I want them to always remain teachable, and to always look for something to learn and someone to learn from," she concluded.

Sarah offers three suggestions for beginners.

First, "It can be very overwhelming. My advice would be to think about your reasons for homeschooling. Think about each child and how they might learn. Would they do better with more reading material, workbooks, or hands-on materials? If you have children close in age, can you combine subjects to cover several grades? Would it work better to have kids separated or working in the same room? Keep it simple."

Second, "There are many resources available. Home School Legal Defense Association is a national organization that is full of resources on legal issues. Ask friends if they know of anyone personally who homeschools. Veteran homeschool moms are incredible resources. Search online for local organizations, co-ops, and groups, and check them out."

Third, "My advice to new homeschoolers is to not jump in full force to every group, organization, or activity that you find available to homeschoolers. Give yourself at least one semester to get your feet wet. It can lead to quick burnout if you have too many irons in the fire, and your schooling at home starts lacking. There are so many cool things out there, but pace yourself."

Study the Example: *Michael and Zack*

There's nothing traditional about the way homeschooling took place with Michael, his wife, and their four kids.

A university professor who holds a PhD, Michael and his son Zack, who is in graduate school, sat down together to talk about how education looked in their household.

"The way most people do homeschooling is too hard, and I think it's wrong," Michael said. "They think it has to be like school, and the mom is usually the teacher. Very few people are equipped to do that. I'd be hard-pressed to cover all the topics.

"Our approach was completely different. We looked specifically for a self-paced curriculum where all of the responsibility for learning was on the child," he said. "All the parent has to do is check to see if the child has achieved milestones along the way. There are quizzes and tests. If you pass, you move on, and if not, you go back to that section again. It's just a matter for the parent to check and see if progress is being made."

Michael does not think use of one specific curriculum over another particularly makes a difference in the educational outcome for a student.

"One of the main mistakes people make is getting into huge discussions that take place in homeschool associations," he said. "I always called it the 'curriculum wars,' because parents would get so competitive, sure that they had found the magic combination. It's crazy. Some are a little better, but all are overall adequate for what you need to do.

"The other part for us is that our children didn't spend very much time with the curriculum," he explained. "On an average over all of the years, I would say they spent maybe an hour and a half per day at it. It was a longer time when they were in high school, and significantly shorter in elementary."

"We spent the rest of the time around the house reading, or doing other stuff we were interested in, like music," Zack said.

The entire process was a little different for Zack, who is the youngest, because the Internet was available for him to pursue topics he was interested in.

"I became interested in music when I was 13, which is late for beginning music," he said, "but because I had all this time, all I did with my free time was music, so I basically caught up. I started with guitar, and now I am producing, writing songs, and recording."

"He learned how to play guitar from watching YouTube videos," Michael said.

"My guitar teacher only taught me songs," Zack said. "All of the music theory I learned with Google and YouTube. That was all I wanted to do."

For his older brother, Joel, computers were a compelling interest.

"My brother quickly became interested in computers and in business," Zack said, "so Dad bought computer parts and Joel built his own computer. He started his first business when he was thirteen years old, and he still makes money from that today."

Joel, now in his thirties, went from building his own computers to scripting and programming. He started a company in Los Angeles, and his career today involves creating apps for clients.

Another son, David, writes for a website and hosts a podcast that reviews films.

The approach that Michael and his wife took to educating their children allowed them to tailor learning to each child's particular personality and needs.

"Teaching our daughter to read was an interesting experience. Faith has the kind of personality that it's simply not possible to *make* her do something," he said.

Research on homeschooling in the early years from a foundation at Stanford University showed that when it came to learning to read, the later students started, the better. They advocated not rushing the process, and that influenced Michael's approach.

"They recommended that if a child wants to read, that's fine, but not to push," he said. "Even if it's as late as eight to ten years old, they'll catch up.

"Faith wasn't interested in kindergarten, or in first grade or second grade," he said. "She was about nine years old and still refusing to read. I took her to dinner one Wednesday night, and then I took her to a comic book store and picked one I thought she might like, about an eight-year-old girl who has adventures in space.

"I read it to her, and the next week I got her another, and then another. Every Wednesday until she was twenty-one, I took her out to eat and to the comic book store," Michael said. "The only reason we stopped was that she went to New York City for a semester for her internship. I went to New York twice that semester, and both times, I took her out to eat and we went to a comic book store.

"She learned to read in three months. It just took the right thing to spark her interest. That was her personality," he said.

Another benefit of homeschooling, Michael believes, is the flexibility that it creates for the content and manner of the lessons.

"We let them play with video games," he said, "because it develops strong hand-eye coordination, and it totally programs kids not to be easily discouraged.

"When I was growing up in school, the number one thing I wanted was to avoid any kind of failure. I seldom got to actually do anything because we spent all of our time preparing—memorizing and studying so you wouldn't fail—and then maybe at some point you actually got to try," Michael said. "But children who grow up playing video games will try anything, and that's actually how you learn stuff. Children learn by playing, until they go to school, and then we ruin it."

"If you do it right, homeschooling is easy to maintain. Observe your child's interests, and feed those. That's what is going to feed your child's motivation to learn and pursue and achieve," he said.

"Homeschool never seemed to us to be mostly about academics," Zack said. "Class was really always in session, but it never felt like it."

Another aspect of homeschooling for the family is the effect it had on relationships within their home.

"One of the main benefits from my point of view is that we avoided the fear of man that most teens seem to automatically get," Michael said. "It's like they can't decide anything unless they know what their friends think."

Zack has noticed that difference, too.

"It's really just now, as I ask my college-age friends about their upbringings, that it's clear to me that my parents are my best friends," he said. "I don't know other kids who went to school who say that, probably because they spent a minority of their time with their family. Their go-to people for discussing issues are not their parents.

"That never happened to me, and I'm glad," he said. "I will definitely homeschool my own kids because if they're going to share their concerns with their friends or with me, I'd want it to be me."

Because his dad's job as a professor and his mom's work as a ballet teacher allowed them each to have their children at work with them often, Zack believes that learning to relate to people happened naturally.

"I would hang out at my parents' work, and I learned to be comfortable with friends of all ages. My whole life I've had college-age friends because they were around, and I took karate lessons," Zack said. "School is artificial socialization. I never felt handicapped talking to anyone."

In his role as a professor, though, Michael has observed that a few homeschoolers do struggle with the change.

"I've had some students who were stereotypical," he said. "They were homeschooled all the way through, with very strict parents. They come to college, and they go nuts.

"I recall one student who had real difficulty in actually doing the classwork," he recalled, "and it seemed to be because of how her homeschool had operated.

"But many, many more, other than the bad examples, have succeeded. I would notice students excelling in some way, and then I would find out that they were homeschooled. There is a much longer list of those. Only a few over the years have been among the spectacular flame-outs," Michael said.

"Because of the flexibility of it, in my opinion there's no inherent weakness in homeschooling; you can always adjust what you're doing," he said.

When it was time to make the transition to the university setting, Zack thinks he was well prepared.

"I didn't even notice," he said, "except for getting up early."

DO YOUR HOMEWORK

Using a Bible-based curriculum to teach our kids to read, and making sure they learn to make and keep friends by participating in sports and activity co-ops with other homeschool families, is good, bedrock stuff for homeschooling. But it is just not enough.

You will find lots of talk in the homeschool community about "socialization," but that should mean much more than helping our children develop the ability to relate to people in our circles and to be comfortable in social situations. It's way more than making sure they have cool haircuts and stylish frames for their glasses. (Although I have to admit that's not a bad idea, unspiritual as that sounds. I still have parent guilt over the bangs I cut for my daughter when she was in sixth grade. Family photos are there to prove my mothering fail, and I still get the "look" from her when the old vacation videos roll.)

As Christ–followers, it should be our goal to emulate his attitudes and actions, living in obedience to his two great commands—to love God and to love people. That is what we want to be teaching our children, as well.

It is right and good to protect our children from whatever would threaten them physically, emotionally, or spiritually. But we also must be consciously preparing them not to fear, but to understand people's needs and motivations, and to respond to all they may meet with God's love, mercy, and grace.

Even as they refrain from participating in any negative behaviors themselves, we need to help them to not judge or be dismissive of people who may not believe or have lifestyles exactly like their own. These are things they will learn from watching you and listening to you at home.

One of the saddest experiences in our work as youth pastors happened when two of our youth group members brought some kids to an activity with them. These were not scrubbed, shiny teens. They were from a rough part of town, where they had a rough existence, and it showed. But they had expressed an interest in knowing more about Jesus, so our youth group kids, rightly, invited them, picked them up, and brought them.

Some of our other youth group kids had been so sheltered that the mere presence of the guests scared them to death. They were frozen, and quite obviously fearful all night long, but to the guests, they came off as judgmental and uninviting.

Even more disturbing was the reaction of some of the parents, later in the week, who complained that they didn't want their own children exposed to "those kids."

Our task as parents is to work to raise kids who are strong in their own faith, and therefore not vulnerable to any perceived threats from being around people who are different from them, but instead who can be Christ-like and welcoming to whomever they encounter.

As homeschool parents, your homework assignment is to be sure that your children know people outside of your church and co-op circles. You will need to help them develop open, kind attitudes toward your neighbors, clerks in stores, the kid with the scary tattoo who's working the window at your fast-food restaurant, and the grouchy old woman who yells at them when their ball sails over her fence.

You can do this in several purposeful ways.

Make it a point to watch local, national, and world news broadcasts together. Talk about why people in the news might act and react the way they do, and think of what their physical, emotional, and spiritual needs might be at the moment. Teach your kids to pray for those people and their needs.

Seek opportunities in your community to serve together as a family. As they work with you, under your protection and supervision, your kids will develop compassion and understanding and will learn to not feel threatened by people whose life stories are different from their own.

In their studies, make it a point to consider the various factors that influence individuals and nations, and talk at length about why, as Christ-followers, your family chooses to live as you do.

Help them, from earliest days through their teen years, to learn to interpret the culture in light of Scripture, and practice with them the ability to interact with all people by following the example of Jesus we see in the New Testament.

In their studies, and in the experiences you design for them, help them learn to approach all of their life in the light of God's calling to his children.

As much as we might want to do so, to insulate our children in Bubble Wrap by keeping them safely within the confines of home and church is to ultimately risk making them adults who cannot rise to the occasions to which a life following Christ will call them.

Homeschooling offers a family unlimited days together and the flexibility to make both academic and spiritual growth times of great adventure for each person. The ultimate challenge for parents, though, no matter what form of schooling we may choose, is to be certain that we are teaching our children to live not by fear, but by faith.

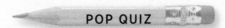

POP QUIZ

1. Looking at my family's goals for educating our children, what aspects of homeschooling would support achieving those goals?

2. What traits of both parents and children, or what particular characteristics of our specific family situation, might work against us if we tried homeschooling? Can we come up with a way to make it work?

OUTSIDE READING

This site has great information for homeschool parents, especially for your start-up. It not only informs you, it inspires you to keep working and trying new ideas.

homeschoolenrichment.com

When you've done all the homeschooling groundwork, and you get down to the real thing, this is a huge help in deciding on a curriculum style and helping you find it. It's specifically for Texas homeschoolers, but this part of the site works for almost everyone. You might see if your state has a similar site.

www.thsc.org/home-school-resources/curriculum/types-of -curriculum

Chapter Four

CHRISTIAN SCHOOL

She was a pastor's wife, and our daughters were best friends.

She had called to tell me she wanted a recipe.

I told her I would make a copy as soon as we finished the project we were working on that night for family devotions.

"Oh," she laughed. "We don't do family devotions. We send the kids to Christian school, and we figure that's enough for one day."

Nope. No, no, and no. Wrong reason for sending your kids to private Christian school. More wrong reasons for choosing private Christian school would include the following:

- "We don't want our kids being exposed to bad kids. You know, drugs, sexual activity, wild parties, evil music."
- "We don't want them to be taught about evolution or global warming or any of that stuff."
- "We want our kids to be good Christians."

As with all the choices, there are some really great reasons to send our children to private Christian school. However, fear that knowing nonbelievers will somehow destroy our kids, or believing in some kind of magical, guaranteed formula that automatically ensures that our kids will be Christians, are not among them.

The lack of effective public schools in a community, or the desire to educate our children from a Christian worldview by exposing them to Christian thought and philosophy and teaching them to examine information in light of Scripture, to prepare them to fulfill God's purpose in their lives—these are sound reasons, and parents in this country have relied on the church in that respect since the colonies were established in the 1600s, giving birth to some of our oldest and most respected colleges and universities.

But because not all families could afford to educate their children, Horace Mann began to advocate offering a free education to all citizens, giving rise to the current system of public education, born in the 1830s.

For nearly a century, public schools in America were not much different from the private schools in format or philosophy, and the Judeo-Christian worldview and narratives were still an overarching framework for content of instruction.

But in the years after World War II, things began to slowly change, and the widening gap between sacred and secular culture became evident in public education as well.

School children in the 1950s and 1960s, for instance, decorated their classrooms and planned pageants at Christmas. In today's public schools, we speak of the "winter break" and keep our decorations to a snowflake theme so that students of all faiths will not feel excluded.

At this time, some parents perceive a hostility toward the Christian faith that prompts them to find a way to educate their children in a setting where their faith is nurtured, and academics are pursued from a decidedly Christian worldview.

Dr. Jake Walters, superintendent of a large and successful Christian school, began our conversation by noting the biggest distinguishing factor of a Christian school today.

"It is a place where the Lord's name is honored, and faith doesn't have to be left at the front gate," he said.

While he acknowledges that there are many "pockets of excellence" among the numerous homeschools and public schools that exist today, he outlines the strengths of a private Christian education.

"There are the obvious ones, like class size and teacher attention, and the freedom from federal restrictions," Walters said. "The most important is that families can put the instructions in Deuteronomy 6 into practice in their child's education. There is never a disconnect as far as education and the practice of their faith goes.

"The strong point about Christian school is that it offers the benefits of homeschool, but with more organization. Children are educated according to the family's beliefs," he said.

In considering the best choice for educating their children, it will be important for parents to invest some time and effort into evaluating the effectiveness of the Christian schools available in their own community.

While the Declaration of Independence holds the truth that all men are created equal as self-evident, when it comes to private Christian schools, the opposite is true. For any parent shopping for the right school for their child, it quickly becomes self-evident that private schools can be as different as night from day.

Remember Your "Why"
A good place to start the decision process is with your list of goals for your child's education.

Keeping these in mind, along with your child's specific needs and abilities, begin by comparing your list to the school's purpose and goals as stated in their printed literature or on their website.

Pay particular attention to understanding whether the emphasis seems to be on perpetuating a specific doctrine or dogma, or on developing a broad base of knowledge and critical-thinking skills for students.

When you find a school whose mission statement and goals appear to line up with your own, put that one on your list for further research. There is really no need to waste your time or theirs on a school whose mission clearly does not line up with yours.

Reality Check

I'm the kind of shopper who looks at the price tag before I try on an outfit because I don't want to fall in love with something I can't afford and then be unhappy with anything less. So this is the point in the process where I would call for a reality check.

The first question addresses your finances. What is the yearly tuition? While there are often payment plans, discounts for multiple students from the same family, and sometimes even scholarships, the bottom line on what you will be paying is extremely important.

If sending your child to a certain school will place you in danger of missing house payments or rent in a month where an unexpected expense could sink your ship, that could be a good indicator that a particular school is not really for you. A quick review of what the Bible has to say about finances and debt would be in order, and having a practical, workable price range in mind ahead of time could aid you in your search.

Some expenses to factor into your education budget would also include uniforms, if required, and any activity fees, textbook or lab fees, and even things like the cost of field trips or retreats or mission trips that might not be included in tuition. These are things to find out ahead of time and include in your consideration of finances.

While I certainly believe that God is a generous, faithful provider to his children, I also believe that he often uses the circumstances he places us in to guide us. I would strongly caution against choosing a school that would cost more than your family can practically afford.

Evaluating Effectiveness

Once you have your short list in hand, it's time to discover the effectiveness of the schools you are considering. While many private Christian schools offer excellence in every aspect, there are sadly others that merely "play school," while adding money to church or personal coffers. There will be many that fall somewhere between the two extremes.

One of the first indicators of excellence you may even find on the school's website: SAT scores, which are significant because all students in all educational situations take the same test.

Walters encourages parents to note the correlation between the average GPA and the SAT scores.

"If they are even, that means that the school is on target with evaluation of students," he explained. "But if the GPA is high, and SAT scores are only mediocre, then perhaps the standard of student achievement in the classroom is set too low."

A school will also indicate that it is accredited and by whom. Many Christian schools maintain accreditation through the Association of Christian Schools International (ACSI).

However, Walters notes that the emphasis on accreditation is changing.

"Colleges don't look at that so much anymore because they are accepting many more applicants from homeschooling," he said. "What they do look at is SAT scores and portfolios of work, which would indicate a standard even higher than what is required for accreditation."

Who's Teaching
Because the standard requirements for teachers can vary greatly from one private school to another, it is extremely important to find out the criteria for hiring classroom teachers for each school you may consider.

Does the school require knowledge of subject matter in the form of a general bachelor's degree, or do they specifically hire teachers trained in instruction and classroom management? Do they accept teachers with a more general education than that? What is the experience level of the faculty?

Walters advises that parents should determine whether faculty members are teaching for test outcomes or for application of critical-thinking skills.

"For example," he said, "a Christian school could totally dismiss discussing climate change, or it could encourage students to research and to think about a topic and draw conclusions, and come up with possible solutions.

"An effective school will avoid dogma in favor of developing students' skills in critical thinking over the long-range faith journey."

Curriculum Counts
Perhaps because of all the commotion and controversy over Common Core, a set of national standards and guidelines that indicate what skills children should have at each grade level and that include some unconventional lessons in basic math among other things, parents are more aware of the actual content and approach to learning in schools than ever before.

Beginning in earliest grades, you will want to know whether your children are learning reading, for instance, using phonics, as with the Abeka curriculum popular with many Christian schools, or the "see-say" word recognition method, or a combination. The same will be true of basic math skills.

As your child progresses, you will want to consider the content of learning, and the methods employed to teach it. This is where your knowledge of your own child's learning style will be valuable, as you look for an environment where your child will thrive.

You should be able to see the curriculum when you make a campus visit, and then you can research online to compare it to your child's needs and abilities.

Other Opportunities

Another key aspect to consider is the range and quality of extra-curricular programs. Will your child be able to pursue interests, develop talents, make friends, and develop things like character, leadership, teamwork, citizenship, commitment, and time management by participating in athletics, music, drama, art, journalism, clubs, or competitive teams?

And to what level are the groups developed? If the athletes participate in a conference, or league, or if the band and choir perform in front of audiences or compete at festivals, then the experience will be richer for your child, but might also require more of a commitment of both time and money on your part.

The same is true of drama, journalism, speech, or debate. Do the students do actual productions, do the yearbook staff members take photos at events and produce a yearbook and online or print newspaper, or do they just meet as an after-school club? And which is a better fit for your student and your family?

Children with Special Needs

It may be a bigger challenge to find a private school that is a great fit if your child has special needs. In fact, some private schools do not accept students with special needs at all. This is not necessarily a matter of discrimination.

"It is often a financial question," Walters explained. "Private schools aren't staffed or equipped to help a special needs child, while public schools are fully equipped and funded."

If you find a private school that accepts students with special needs, ask to see the facilities and speak with the teachers, and ask to be put into contact with other parents whose special needs students are part of the program.

I will never forget the day a friend who had just taken a job teaching at a Christian school was showing me the school.

"We even have a special needs class!" she exclaimed, opening the door to that classroom.

I saw an eight-by-twelve-foot room with no window, pretty obviously converted from a storage closet, where seven special needs students and their teacher, who had no special training, would spend their days. I felt sick with dismay for those kids and the teacher, especially when only a few blocks away, the public elementary school had trained teachers and every resource each child would need, at no expense to the parents.

The Campus Visit

Most private schools will encourage you to visit the campus for a tour, where they obviously will be showcasing their facilities.

If at all possible, parents need to walk the halls on a normal day when school is in session, bringing their child along, too.

While you should coach your child to try to picture himself walking the halls, or picture himself in the classrooms, and see how he thinks he would fit in, there are several indicators parents can note.

As you walk through the facilities, look into each classroom you pass and try to judge the level of engagement of both the teacher and the kids.

A classroom that is totally silent, unless there is testing, might not be as effective as one where there is some talking and movement, and even laughter.

Check on the adequacy of science and computer labs, and ask to see the library. Pay attention to what you see displayed in classrooms and halls, even at the secondary level. True learning is busy and noisy and even a little messy.

For the best experience, academically and spiritually, the student body should reflect diversity both ethnically and economically. Be conscious of that.

In a Christian school, there should be evidence of an emphasis on teaching character and moral and spiritual values.

Some of that will show up as you walk the halls, but parents may need to look a little more closely, too. Walters recommends that families try to attend school-wide events, like a baseball game or a fine arts performance, of schools they are considering.

"You can't have a great school without order," he said. "The curriculum of a school is what is taught in the halls, as well as from the curriculum guide. The behavior of the students, the respect and honor they exhibit, are outward symbols of what is taught in the classrooms.

"Go to a game. How the athletes act, the interaction and attitudes of the parents and the crowd speaks volumes," he said.

"In fact," he continued, "before I accepted my position at this school, I went to a football game and sat in the stands. It was a hard-fought one, and both teams played well, but in the last minutes, the receiver missed a perfect pass that would have been the winning score.

"As I headed across the field after the game, I saw the quarterback go over and put his arm around that receiver's shoulders, and I heard him say, 'Richard, there are other games. You did your best.' That was when I knew that this school was effectively teaching all of the right things for the right reasons, and I decided to take the job."

After spending time on campus, ask your child, even as a preschooler, to tell you what they observed, both positive and negative, and share your ideas and impressions with your child. Ask your student, "Can you see yourself there?" And ask the same question of yourself.

Avoid Unrealistic Expectations

As positive as an education at an excellent private Christian school may be, there are some misconceptions that Dr. Walters thinks can lead to a disappointing experience for some families.

"There can be unrealistic expectations from parents sometimes," he said. "We can never replace the role that a parent plays spiritually, emotionally, or in discipline and training in a child's life. We can support and be partners, but we can't fill the parent's shoes.

"We also cannot reform a child with deep problems," he said. "Again, we might be able to support the parents' efforts, but that is not the purpose for which we are here."

With so much to consider, and a significant investment of money involved, choosing to send your children to a private Christian school is a challenge, and then selecting the exact school adds even more to the task. However, Walters offered one last reminder to parents struggling with the decision.

"It's not going to be the end of the world if you discover you made a mistake," he said. "After all, you are not really doing anything that can't be undone if the need arises."

And, as we've said before, armed with research and information combined with diligent prayer, parents can rely on God to surely guide them as they seek direction.

Study the Example: *Ellen and Classical Education*

My husband and I had been asked to speak at a parent training conference for a private Christian school, and we were scheduled to meet with administrators to begin planning.

Our direction to the office took us down hallways as classes were in session, and the teacher in me couldn't help but slow down and glimpse as much as I could of what was going on in the classrooms as we passed by.

I was highly impressed and deeply encouraged by what I saw happening there, from elementary grades through the middle school classrooms on that hallway.

In every room I observed a high level of activity and student engagement. Students were working in groups, and they were active in discussion or question-and-answer that was moving quickly. I was struck by the eagerness among the students, noticeable even in the quick walk-by from the hall. I whispered to my husband, "Wow! These kids are really learning!"

Over the several days of the conference, various middle school and high school students were assigned to be our assistants. They were without fail respectful, cheerful, and helpful young people. But they further impressed me with their easy confidence and ability to interact with us, adults they had just met. We had great spontaneous conversations about literature, history, their hopes for college and careers, and by the end of the conference, I felt the need to figure out what it was that was making this school so clearly excellent.

And that's how I became interested in two models for private education that have been gaining ground since the 1990s.

The first, called classical education, concerns curriculum and the approach to learning. How this is organized specifically can vary from school to school, but in general, there are three phases.

In kindergarten through fourth grade, called the grammar phase, there is emphasis on the memorization of facts, from the times tables and facts about nature to vocabulary. This may also include the beginning study of Latin, which can continue throughout the students' education.

In fifth through eighth grades, students progress to the logic phase, where they begin to exercise independent thinking by ordering facts to support their "arguments," whether in history, science, literature, or math.

And finally, high school students will move into the rhetoric phase, where the focus is on the ability to communicate concepts and academic arguments effectively to others.

Throughout the grades, curriculum usually includes the study of classical art, music, and literature.

The classical model can be found in some public schools and academies, and there are numerous Christian schools employing a specifically Christian classical curriculum. Homeschooling parents also are purchasing that curriculum.

The other model, which is more about the organization and logistics of the school, is called the university model. University-Model Schools International (UMSI) is made up of Christian schools whose aim is to equip parents for their role as primary encouragers in their children's faith. The curriculum can be classical or traditional.

Ellen Schuknecht, a career educator and one of the founders of Veritas Academy in Austin, Texas, explained to me how the two models combined work there.

"School is a tool for helping students achieve a high standard of academics," she said, "but the parent is the key influence. The major difference is that this model creates time for parents to own that piece. Character and spiritual development happen primarily at home. What happens there is what really gets into a child's heart."

The schedule, which Schuknecht says is difficult for a family with two working parents to implement, develops over time until older students are following a traditional college schedule.

At her school, students in kindergarten through fourth grade attend school two full days a week, and home assignments, intended for parent leadership, are given for the other three days.

In fifth grade, students begin to attend class on Monday, Wednesday, and Friday, with work for parents to oversee on the other two days.

Eighth graders follow a college schedule, with some classes meeting on Monday, Wednesday, and Friday, and others meeting on Tuesday and Thursday.

High school students follow the college structure and have the option to be on campus all day, participating in extracurriculars or study groups.

"We find that because of this schedule, our students thrive when they get to college," Schuknecht said.

While the parent role is important in this model, it is distinctively not homeschooling.

"We dictate the curriculum, the pacing, and the standards," she explained. "We are a college prep school with high academic standards, and parents are engaged in the process, but by high school, when the students are on a college schedule, parents are not so involved in the academics, but are still crucial in the spiritual training."

For the model to work well, more and more ownership of learning is offered to the child until the child is totally responsible for the learning, with the parent there to guide and offer support as needed.

"The parent role is key, but it evolves," Schuknecht said. "In elementary school, they act as teachers, in middle school they become a guided tutor, and by high school they are the student's cheerleader. A lot more is expected of the parent early on, and some parents struggle a little because they want to hold onto that teacher role. But because we have college readiness instruction, the goal for high school students is really more of a one-on-one mentorship between parent and child. We want the kids to own the process and not need to be spoon-fed."

The university-model concept developed out of a desire of parents who came to realize that just because they had their kids in Sunday school or Christian school, it didn't necessarily mean that the heart of that child had been touched, according to Schuknecht.

"Sunday school develops a head-knowledge of the faith, but not necessarily a heart-knowledge. These parents were desiring a bigger role in the process, knowing that one-on-one at home is where character is built.

"The distinctive aim of our school is reaching the hearts of our kids to own their faith. We want to see them making the effort, learning to do their best, and aiming for excellence as they grow in the skills God has given them," she said.

Study the Example: *Andy*

Andy, who holds a master's degree in education, teaches reading to middle school students in one of the leading school districts in Texas and is in demand as a speaker and clinician at educator workshops.

But for us, Andy is a voice of experience on the different choices parents have for schooling their kids, because growing up he did it all. More than once.

"I didn't go to the same school two years in a row until high school," he said.

In first grade, he was homeschooled; in second grade, he was part of a Christian homeschool co-op group; and in third grade, he attended public school. Fourth grade was homeschooled, fifth was back in public school, and sixth was in a different public school for the first half of the year.

"Then for the last part of the year, I was back in homeschool because my parents thought I was getting too rowdy," he chuckled. He started seventh grade in homeschool, but attended public school for the last half of that year.

Beginning in eighth grade, he attended public school through high school. He attended a public university for one year and then transferred to a private Christian university to complete his bachelor's degree.

"Bouncing around affected me in a lot of ways," Andy recalled. "I didn't have friends for very long, which was tough, but it made it easier for me to get into a new school and know what to expect, and how to relate to others. When I was being homeschooled, I was never by myself because my sisters were always there, too."

Because his mom was a certified teacher, homeschool at Andy's house had definite structure.

She broke up the day into different class times, setting a timer for forty-five minutes. For instance, during the math time, each of her three children would be working on that subject, but from different books.

"For science, she got us lab packets, and we would do soda-and-vinegar-type experiments," Andy said. "We had reading time and Bible study, and we would go on bike rides or walk the dog for P.E., and that was pretty much it."

The biggest part of the day was the two hours set aside for reading whatever the kids wanted.

"We'd go to the library and pick out books," Andy said. "Also, every day my mom would read out loud to us, even until we were in seventh grade. That was probably the best thing about homeschool. We'd go on reading field trips to the park. We'd sit on a blanket, and mom would read to us. That made me a better reader, and it made me close to my family."

But there were drawbacks from homeschooling for Andy, as well.

"The worst part of being homeschooled was that I had no friends," he recalled. "I was with my two sisters, but none of my friends were in my homeschool groups, and I didn't have a brother yet, so I felt a little cramped at home.

"I always liked going back to public school because then I could be with my friends and other kids. I feel like I was a little behind socially up until high school."

He particularly felt this as an adolescent, learning to relate to girls.

"I had awkward run-ins with girls because I didn't know how to act, maybe up until I was in college," Andy said. "I was good at talking to my sisters and my mom but not so good at flirting."

Moving to public school had its disadvantages academically, however.

"The downfall of public school for me was that because of all the work we had done in homeschool, and all of the reading, I was way advanced. I was so far ahead of where my peers were that school was more of a social learning place, which I definitely needed, than academic learning," he explained.

"As we grew older, all of us kids grew out of my mom's expertise in math and science, so that by seventh grade she kind of gave us the text and said, 'Well, do your best.'

"I struggled in math when I would go back to public school, and then I was behind in eighth and ninth grade. Even though I was in honors classes, I was never that strong because I think I had missed out on stuff," Andy said. "Reading and English were always where I excelled because Mom had given me the freedom and time to read whatever I wanted."

Andy started college as a pre-med student at Boise State University (where he had even played a high school football game on that famous blue field), mostly because he thought he could make a lot of money as a doctor. But at the end of his freshman year, he changed his plan and transferred to a Christian college.

"The summer after my freshman year, I read a lot of really good books," he said. "I realized that this was what I wanted to do.

"So I decided to transfer to the Christian college in the neighborhood where I grew up, and I could go to my old church with my friends, which was kind of a safety net. I also wanted a Christian college because I felt like it would support my growth in my faith."

Having now taught in public schools for seven years, Andy has some comparisons that have influenced his conclusions about the different choices for schooling.

"I had cousins and many friends at church who only attended private Christian schools, but I think that for me public school was the best route because of the many resources that kids are offered through athletics and extracurriculars," he said.

"I never got to do sports until high school. Once a year, I got to participate in our church's drama production, but I would have loved to be in theatre in school. There were activities that I would have enjoyed that I missed out on just because I think my parents were afraid of the impact that public school would have on me.

"But teaching public school, I see that kids getting to interact with others from all different sorts of backgrounds is a positive aspect," Andy said. "Students learning to work together with kids from widely different backgrounds, and with different personalities, is the most valuable part of education because they are learning how to interact with the world they will be working in someday.

"People skills are crucial, and that is where I was lacking, coming from homeschool. It took until I was in college to become confident."

Meanwhile, Andy charts his spiritual journey as it relates to his educational one.

"I was always a really good church kid, on all of the leadership teams," he said. "Church was stable. Even though I was transferring schools, I went to the same church for eight years, through junior high, which kept me grounded.

"But at public school, I kept the church world and the school world and the home world all separate in my mind."

They didn't really mix until Andy began attending public high school.

"I got involved in Fellowship of Christian Athletes in high school, but in elementary and junior high, I just tried to do what was cool to the cool kids at school," he said.

"In my head, I wanted to do what was right," Andy recalled. "Like in junior high, I went through this phase of making marks on my arm with a pen every time I said a bad word, so that I'd remember to apologize for it later. I just really wanted to be cool at school.

"There was only one year where I was at a public school with kids from my church, so I mostly felt on my own, and church was a different thing. If I look at my sixth grade self from a faith perspective, I was struggling," he said.

A key point for Andy came when his parents allowed him to make the decision on where he would attend eighth grade.

"I had the opportunity to go to a Christian middle school," he said. "We went and toured the school, where a couple of my friends went. Then I sat down with my parents and they said, 'Okay, do you want to do this, or do you want to go back to public school?' I felt like I had a lot of power in that conversation. My thoughts actually mattered."

Allowed to make the choice, Andy decided he wanted to attend public school.

"Part of my reason was because the Christian school required uniforms," he said, "but also Christian school seemed like church 2.0. I would go to church and do Awana (an international discipleship program) and youth group. The school had chapel, and it seemed like the same thing over again, so I wanted to go to a different environment."

Looking back, Andy has thought about how his choices of school may have impacted his spiritual life.

"I don't think it would have mattered if I had gone to Christian middle and high school," he said. "I don't think I would have been a 'better Christian.' I would have turned out just the same.

"Or, it might have made me more angry to go to a Christian school," he continued. "I liked youth group, but in Awana I hated all the rules and restrictions. It seemed really legalistic, so going to a school like that might have driven me further away. I'm glad

I didn't go to the Christian school. For me at that time, church was enough."

After a year at a state university, though, Andy transferred to Biola University, a Christian school.

"It was a personal choice to move to a Christian college," Andy said. "I took out all the loans, and I did the applications. My parents had nothing to do with it. That was when I started to really grow a lot. At that point, I was able to understand more what my personal salvation is and what my role in the community is."

As a career educator, Andy has drawn some thoughtful conclusions about the roles that school and home play in students' lives.

"I was thinking about it today, as I walked through the halls before school, saying hi to some of my kids," he said. "I think for the ones who have a strong homelife, no matter what school they go to, it's not going to do that much damage. But for the kids who don't have a good homelife, school can either help them get out of that, or it can set them back even further.

"So the kids who already do things with their parents and their families at home are going to be fine, no matter what school they attend. But for others, if the family is not strong, it can make all the difference," he said. "Your kids are going to value what you value, so you have to demonstrate those values that you want them to take as their own."

Study the Example: Joy

When it comes to insight born of experience, Joy's is a voice parents can learn from.

With her master's degree in education, and time teaching in both private Christian schools and public schools, she not only has perspective from the teacher's side of the desk, but she is also the mom of three children who have attended both public and private Christian schools at various times.

Joy's journey as an educator began as she was volunteering in the church preschool where her son was enrolled.

"The church's academy needed a science teacher, and they hired me," she said. "I immediately went online and looked at what other science teachers at private schools were doing. That became the foundation of my teaching philosophy because I picked up the concept of teaching and caring about the whole child and the importance of the relationship with the child and their parents."

Based on her five years as a teacher at a private Christian school, Joy sees one area that parents looking for such a school should be concerned with exploring specifically.

"I think that academic rigor in Christian education should be looked at more," she said. "In the Bible, for example, Daniel was familiar with the ways of his world, so his testimony had credibility. Paul, too, understood the culture and spoke the language, so he was able to speak to the people on Mars Hill with great effect."

As a military family, Joy and her husband have moved more than once, going through the process of both deciding on schools for their children and accepting teaching positions for her. She made the transition to teaching in a Title I public high school, where 62 percent of her students are economically disadvantaged, by first substituting in public schools.

"I fell in love with my students, even though their situations and circumstances shocked me," she said. "The socio-economic circles that my family lived and worshipped in never intersected with the circles where I teach, so my perspective was not from lived experience. My eyes were opened. I had read about such schools, but I hadn't experienced it. The level of things my students deal with was beyond my understanding.

"But I was studying for my master's degree at a Christian university, where the head of the school of education had a true mission focus for public schools. So when I was offered a job at the public high school, and I sought his input, he said, 'Go!'

"I love my job," Joy said. "Both my experience at the Christian academy and my time teaching fourth grade at a Title I elementary school prepared me. They each helped me see where the students are coming from, and how to teach the whole child."

When it came to placing her children in a pre-K, Joy took into consideration the results of research that indicate that certified teachers and smaller class sizes that allow all the students to have a more personal level of attention are most effective in setting youngsters on their path of learning.

"The pre-K my son is in now is the nicest in this area, with people coming from miles around. It is the feeder for a prominent and wealthy private school, and for a prominent Christian school, where most families have lots of money," she said. "That private Christian school has both strong academic rigor and a strong Christian focus. You don't always see that. Some schools are strong on the Christian focus, but not academically. If we were to go the private route with my oldest, she would definitely go to an accredited ACSI [Association of Christian Schools International] school, where the rigor is strong."

At different times, each of Joy's children has been in public or private schools, based on what is best for that child.

"There was one year where we had all three kids at different schools, with three different drop-off and pick-up times," she said. "That was a hard year for me, but it was best for each of the kids at that time."

In the community where the family is stationed, Joy's daughter was able to attend a nearby public school that was a good fit.

"It was a small, award-winning elementary school. It turns out that the administrators were Christian, and every teacher she had there was a Christian," she said. "Now, she is attending a public middle school, and that can be a little scary sometimes.

"But I agree with what Dr. Tom Kimmel says in one of his books. He says that we don't want to bring our kids up in what he refers to as 'cocoon Christianity.' He believes that faith that is never tested is weak faith, and my husband and I tend to agree.

"So you do have things in public school that kids are exposed to, and we've already had some conversations with our daughter. But I am certain that she's not going to be shocked when she gets to college because she has already been challenged."

But again, Joy pointed out the importance of letting individual family needs and circumstances guide parents' decision.

Making Assumptions

Based on her experiences as both a parent and a teacher, Joy points out some faulty assumptions that parents can make in the process of decision-making.

Christian Schools

🍎 Assuming that a Christian school is automatically a safe place

"Just because your child is in a Christian school, you can't assume that they will have no temptations. There will be kids there that have drugs, or do other harmful things, or even commit suicide," Joy said. "Some parents have their kids there as a shield, but others may use it as a last dumping ground for their kids who have been expelled from public school."

◆ Assuming that the school will take care of the spiritual development of their children

> "While the school staff can support what parents are doing, the first responsibility for the spiritual training of children lies with the parent," Joy said.

◆ Assuming that the level of instruction at a Christian school won't be as rigorous as that of other schools

> "That depends on the individual school," Joy said.

Homeschooling

◆ Assuming that the quality of instruction will not be high or that students will be lacking in socialization skills

> "I have a dear friend who educated all three of her daughters at home, with wonderful results," Joy said. "They were in the Air Force and knew that they would be moving every two years. Even though they knew that there were more opportunities for positive experiences and a breadth of activities in public school, they did not want to be making their girls change schools every two years. For them, everything worked out perfectly. Two of those girls are currently in law school, and they are beautifully socialized, which shows that there really is no 'only way' to do it."

Public Schools

◆ Assuming no one can talk about God

> "I teach science," Joy said, "and my students ask me about God. We can express our faith, and my kids talk about God all the time. I teach at a public magnet

school for the arts, and we pull students from all over the community. With the emphasis on the arts and humanities, the school is sensitive to freedom of expression. Our administration had addressed the gender-specific bathroom question before it was ever in the news.

"We have a number of strong Christian clubs, and the day after a student had killed herself, there were prayer circles filling all of the halls. We have a moment of silence every morning.

"And when the kids ask me what my 'private personal belief' is about a subject, I can and do answer the question."

🍎 Assuming that teachers can't teach character and morals

"Actually," Joy said, "that is part of what is expected."

Major Considerations

Joy thinks that there are four major considerations for parents to think and pray about as they work through the process of choosing a school.

Personal Investment at Home

"It's important to consider how the school will be able to partner with you," Joy said. "As a family, what can you give to the process? If your church has a strong youth program, and if your family has a strong foundation in faith, then your child can probably be okay at a public school. But if not, and if you can't support their spiritual training at home, perhaps because you are new to it, then maybe your child should go to a Christian school for that foundation of faith."

The Nature of Your Child

"If your child, or you as a parent for that matter, require more personal attention, then a private school, or a smaller public school, would be a great choice," Joy explained. "We moved our son out of a perfectly wonderful private preschool because he needed organization and more individual attention than they were able to offer. It would have been easier to leave him there, but we had to move him. At the new school, he got that attention, so at five years old, when we told him we were going to move to Virginia, his response was, 'That was one of the 13 original colonies!' He thrived in public school, but again, you have to know your child to make that decision.

"Some kids would be fine in either situation," Joy continued. "I'm glad we did it all with our daughter. From attending private Christian school early, we later moved her to the [military] base school, which was a good transition because while all of the kids there were not Christian, they were from military families, and the behavioral expectations were high. Now, in public middle school, she's doing great, and she has friends who practice all different religions, which we think is good for her."

Academic Rigor and Preparation

"I'm not sure if people have a good idea of where we're moving globally and economically," Joy said, "but the same skills that parents were taught are not necessarily the same skills needed for the twenty-first century, which includes social skills and high academic standards.

"Faith is important, but our kids also need the knowledge to be prepared for the world they'll be a part of."

Supportive Administration

It is important that the administration be able to provide support for both the students and the parents.

"When we knew that our daughter would attend the public school, I wrote an email to the administrator," Joy said. "I introduced our family and told a little bit about us, and then I asked a question. 'Are you and the faculty team prepared, equipped, and dedicated to partnering with me? You will be with them more hours in the day than I will, and I want to be sure that you're as concerned about their character as you are about their test scores.'

"I got a great letter back," she said. "And when a new administrator took over, I went to an event designed to let parents meet him. I asked the same questions, in person, not realizing that it was the superintendent standing beside him. He was a little taken aback, but he answered my questions. They are now putting together a community advisory panel, and they have asked me to be a part of it, so that demonstrates what they value."

Final Thoughts from Joy

Though there is much to think and pray about, Joy points out that as parents consider what is best for each child, they might come to the understanding that the choice they make now might not always be the same for the child's entire education.

"I know a family who made the conscious decision to homeschool their children through middle school and then send them to public high school," she said. "The mom wanted her kids to have their faith tested before they got to college, and she raised them with the idea that when they got to high school, they would be ambassadors for Christ. She saw it as a way of giving back to the community.

"That mom was mindful that hers were not the only children out there. She trained missionaries, teaching them that school is their mission field. They did well."

DO YOUR HOMEWORK

If there were surefire formulas in our lives as Christ-followers, we wouldn't need grace, we wouldn't need the Holy Spirit, and faith itself would be pretty cheap.

Putting our kids in Christian school is not a surefire formula that will result in all of our children being perfect little church peeps for the rest of their lives.

And really, that's not exactly what we're going for anyway, I hope.

No, what we really, really want is for our kids to come to know and love Jesus, and live out their own unique relationship with him in their own way.

So while sending them to a Christian school can certainly get them off to a good start, it's just not enough to write that tuition check and then fist-pump our way to Starbucks, where we can delete "raise kids in knowledge of the Lord" from the notes on our phone. Sorry, Mom and Dad. You *still* have homework. Maybe even more than the kids do!

Remember those course titles in your major in college that always ended in the description "theory and practice"? That's what we're talking about here.

At school, in chapel, and in Bible classes, your kids are getting theory.

But the practice part is up to you.

It will be crucial that your kids, from tiny to teens, observe their parents living out their faith from day to day. The way you and your spouse relate to one another, in the good moments and particularly when the pressure is on, says more than any family devotional book you could read to them.

The kindness and the grace that you demonstrate toward each other, toward your kids, and toward friends and coworkers is how they will learn to apply those Christ-like characteristics in their own relationships.

Teaching your children a sense of the social responsibility of believers will be your assignment, too, and this is another area where talk is cheap. Especially because at school, at church, and at home, they will only be around people who share the same values and live the same lifestyle, it's going to be important to arrange opportunities for the entire family to gain a sense of the hurts and needs of others in the world.

It will be truly important to do things as a family like volunteering at your local food bank, preparing care bags of things like granola bars and socks for homeless people in your community, or filling an extra backpack with school supplies and dropping it off at a Title I elementary school in your town. And when you do, spend some time afterward talking about the people you met and how much Jesus loves them.

Help them understand the world they live in. They have to see your leadership and active participation in living a Spirit-led life that carries the love of Christ beyond their cozy home and classrooms.

The gift of a private school education that you are giving them, often at a sacrifice, will be wasted if you don't also help them learn how to take it with them to affect the world they live in.

You get the picture. This is still a "no coasting" zone.

Extra Credit: ✓
Go Off Script to Make Learning Lively

Did you do your homework? Let me see.

You got number 5 wrong. The answer should be 9, not 7.

Do you want me to ask you the study questions for the test?

How could you only get a C on this spelling test? We went over the list the night before!

No electronics until your homework is done.

Get busy on your homework.

You have to finish your homework before practice.

Do your homework!

Why did you wait until now to work on that project? The store closes in 15 minutes!

In many homes on any given school night, this is the script for parents whose golden intention is to be active and supportive in seeing to it that their children succeed in school.

It can look the same way for many who homeschool, as well:

Did you finish that chapter? Show me the worksheet.

You need to do the online test by the end of the day.

Finish breakfast, and get two online lessons in history and one in math done by lunch.

But sadly, as well intentioned and dedicated as these parents may be, they are not only missing the point of educating their children, but they are missing precious, fleeting opportunities to build deep and rich relationships with them, as well.

Whether we teach our children at home or send them to school, we need to support and encourage their learning by participating with them.

This absolutely does not mean doing homework or completing projects for them, and it certainly doesn't mean hanging over the Parent Portal and sending annoying emails to their teachers twice a week.

It does mean taking an interest in the actual subjects they are studying, and adding to what is happening during school hours by engaging and broadening their experiences as a family.

Education is about making connections and being able to draw conclusions and make applications to everyday life.

So if your child is learning the geography of Southeast Asia, go online together to Google Earth and zoom in on that area. Hover over a major city, zoom in, and switch to street view. Work together to prepare a meal that includes cuisine of that area, or visit a restaurant where you can sample such dishes. If you know someone who has lived or traveled extensively in that area, invite them to share the meal, and talk about their experiences, show their photos, share souvenirs, and so on. Go to the library and check out literature set there or written by native writers. Rent a movie set there. Visit an art exhibit featuring work from that area, or listen to some native music. Do these things as a family, and talk about it all as you go.

As you demonstrate your own enthusiasm for and interest in exploring new ideas, and share the experience of learning with your kids, you will be cultivating in them a love for education and modeling for them the method for study and the joy of discovery.

You will find that you are also building personal connections with your kids that cement your relationships, as well.

Of course you can't enrich every lesson in such detail, but if you can do it for even one subject, or several times over a school year, you will be influencing your child's learning for a lifetime.

Get off that tired old "Did you do your homework?" script, and act out adventures in education with your child!

 POP QUIZ

1. What aspects of private Christian schools seem most appealing as the choice for our child at this point?

2. What do we recognize right away as some challenges that we would need to deal with to make this choice?

OUTSIDE READING

The Association of Christian Schools International (ACSI) offers a great introduction to private schools. It provides answers and suggests resources for making the decision on a private school education. ACSI is one of several large private school organizations that serve families and schools around the world.

www.acsi.org

The National Association of Independent Schools is not exclusively for Christian schools. Their site gives some great in-depth information regarding private schools.

www.nais.org/Pages/default.aspx

This is a helpful article in considering whether private school is for your child.

www.privateschoolreview.com/blog/the-private-school -advantage-the-top-reasons-to-send-a-child-to-private-school

This site offers a great tool to start with when you're comparing schools.

www.privateschoolreview.com/compare-schools

Here's some helpful information from money people as you consider how to finance tuition.

www.bankrate.com/finance/life-stages/can-you-afford -private-school-1.aspx

When it's time to start doing school visits, these sites can help you prepare.

www.privateschoolreview.com/blog/5-questions-you-need -to-ask

www.greatschools.org/gk/articles/the-school-visit-what-to -look-for-what-to-ask/

If Ellen's example piqued your interest in classical schools, here are some resources you might like to look at.

www.classicalacademicpress.com/what-is-classical-education/

www.welltrainedmind.com/a/classical-education/

For more information about the university model, visit the UMSI website.

umsi.org

Need some help with your homework? My coauthored book *Let It Shine: Partnering with God to Raise World Changers* is full of easily doable ideas for activities, conversation starters, and projects for the whole family that will help you put your family's faith into practice.

Chapter Five

PUBLIC SCHOOL

The first thing we need to do in our discussion of public school as a possibility is clear the air.

Fear is a terrible reason to do or not do anything, yet it seems that too many Christian parents never even consider public school because they are afraid. They fear a "secular" curriculum; they fear ungodly teachers, administrators, counselors, and school boards; they fear that the other kids will lead their children down the path of evil and ruin.

So let's start by addressing such fears.

From Old Testament to New Testament, words to the effect of "fear not" appear 365 times. That's like once a day, every day of the year. In 1 Timothy 1:7, it tells us clearly that fear is not from God, but rather he gives us power, love, and a "sound mind." Fear forbids. Faith invites.

Some parents fear the public school curriculum. But a study of facts in science, math, and history can teach Christian kids in public school to research and evaluate for themselves, a practice that will serve them well in their lives. God and his Word stand up to scrutiny, and based on the number of times in Scripture he asks men to search, seek, ask, and try, questions don't bother God. In fact, searching Scripture for answers to honest questions can make students more firm in their faith, especially when the day's lessons and kid's questions become part of dialogue and Bible study that week at home. In the process of determining where our children will be educated, parents need not be fearful that their children will be spiritually harmed by academic challenge, as long as we are committed to participating in the process with them.

Some parents automatically dismiss public school as an option because they fear the negative influence of teachers, administrators, or counselors who are not spiritually, or even politically, in agreement with them. These well-meaning parents are nevertheless operating on a mistaken assumption. In my experience both as a teacher and a parent, I have found that, in Texas at least, public education is full of moral, caring people, many of whom are also Christ-followers. At every school where I taught, and at each school my kids attended, we were able to participate in prayer groups where we found encouragement, and where we were able to pray specifically for the people and the needs of that school and community. We were certainly not the only ones among the faculty, administrators, or students who saw the school as our mission field, and we recognized that our family had a divine opportunity to pray for the students, the staff, and the larger community, and to support and love them, and demonstrate grace.

Fear of other children being a negative influence is another reason some will shy away from even investigating public school. Whether your school is in an affluent area or one in economic distress, or anywhere in between, remember that stereotypes are not reality. The idea that we can protect our children and surround them with innocence by sending them to Christian school or by keeping them at home is a deeply flawed assumption. Though our daughter attended the Title I public high school where I was teaching, she was in her freshman year at a Christian college before she was ever pressured by friends to drink. She was shocked and disappointed when her roommate, the daughter of missionaries, and another girl backed her into the closet in their dorm room one night, trying to force whiskey down her lips. And of all the friends our son ever brought home from the same high school, it was a homeschooled friend who tried to sneak alcohol into his room and who took our son, though he was unaware of the purpose until they arrived at the house, to meet a drug dealer.

Wherever we feel directed to educate our children, we will have to be vigilant in knowing our children and maintaining strong lines of communication with them, and work to ensure that they see us living out our faith, our love, and our caring about the needs of others.

I know more than one Christian family that has, by their involvement, changed the atmosphere and level of success of an entire school and community. These people not only enrolled their children, but then did all within their power to make a difference. The parents became active in PTA, volunteered to tutor, and invited other children and parents to their home socially. They shared parenting ideas, helped some parents work on job interview skills, and babysat for single moms who had two jobs or who were getting job training they needed. They helped provide for the students who needed school supplies, or coats, or weekend meals. In every case that I know of, the overall academic performance of the students improved, as did discipline, behavior, and parent participation on that campus. And they all can tell stories about students, parents, or teachers who asked them about their relationships with Jesus, or about where they attended church.

One more thing to ponder when speaking of fearing the effect of public school: If people who don't know Jesus, and don't know to seek Jesus, won't be coming to your church, how will they experience grace and redemption if we who do know hide in a bunker and keep all the salt and all the light and all the love to ourselves? We have only to look at the life of Jesus to observe that he went where people were.

Fears aside, it's time now to move our discussion to an honest evaluation of public school education.

The most important thing to know is that public schools vary wildly, not only from district to district, but from one school to another within a district. So you will want to get to know the schools within your own attendance area.

Overall, public education is facing struggles, with an overemphasis on high stakes testing, controversy over some curriculum content within the "common core" that many states are adopting, and attempts to maintain academic standards and discipline within the classroom often stymied by legal restraints.

At some schools, this will have resulted in low staff morale, unchecked student behavior, and classroom instruction that is rote and uninspired.

But this is not the case in all schools. There are still many public schools where the administration ensures that there is order, discipline, and a positive environment in which students learn and succeed, and where teachers have the expertise and the enthusiasm to both instruct and inspire their students.

In most public schools, students have access to materials and programs that enrich the curriculum, with the opportunity to explore interests and develop abilities in music, art, theater, computer skills, and athletics, beginning in elementary school, and continuing with increased depth through high school. Student participation in sports, or organizations like band, drama, debate team, student council or newspaper staff, creates opportunities for students to develop skills in time management, teamwork, responsibility, and interpersonal relationships that serve them well as adults.

In addition to learning socialization, Christian students in public schools can use their experiences there to become prepared to effectively operate in the world outside of the church walls, and may be able to have a spiritual impact on what can be viewed as their mission field.

Parents who become active through PTA or serving on parent committees will find that they earn a voice that can positively affect the entire community.

The variables are so great, however, from state to state and even from school to school, that parents must be diligent in researching the climate and effectiveness of the specific school their children would attend.

You will find some helpful guides for evaluating a public school in the Outside Reading sidebar, and these days every school will have a website. Also know that you can make an appointment to interview the principal, and some districts will allow you to get a visitor pass and eat in the cafeteria, where you can observe the general atmosphere, the interactions of students and teachers on duty, and the interactions of students with one another. There is also the opportunity at most public schools for you to volunteer as a tutor or mentor weekly or monthly, which is a good way to take the pulse of the school, observe what is happening in classrooms and hallways, and contribute to your educational community at the same time. Most PTA organizations welcome membership from community members who do not have a student actually enrolled at the time.

Another good tactic is to talk to a number of parents whose kids actually attend the school, and even to students who are graduates or who are currently enrolled.

On a personal note, I spent the first four and the last twenty-seven years of my forty-three-year teaching career on high school campuses where the students not only struggled daily with the issues that poverty brings but also where the school had a reputation of being dangerous or "rough." But whenever adults from outside would come onto campus, as mentors or speakers, or as sales reps for school pictures or yearbook companies, they would always exclaim over the respectful, positive, helpful attitudes they experienced in every student they encountered. The vast majority of students I taught were bright, kind, hard-working young people who every day overcame challenges that many of us could never imagine, and who did so with great courage and grace. These same kids went on to work their way through college and are now successful, even noted, in their fields, and they are the first to volunteer and give back to their communities.

I say all of that to make this point: if public school is an option you are considering, it is vital that you invest the time and effort to find out for yourself what the situation is at the specific school your kids would be attending.

And a word of encouragement for parents who find, for whatever reason, that they really have no choice but to enroll their children in their nearby public school: God is there, as he is everywhere, and he will protect, and bless, and use your children and you in mighty ways if you allow it. Ask him to direct you and your kids to the administrators, teachers, children, and parents who are Christ-followers, too. You may be surprised at how many you find, and at the ways you can support and encourage one another, as well as at the impact you can have for good in your community.

Study the Example: *Jana*

Jana started life in Germany, where her parents were missionaries. But the summer before she started kindergarten, her family moved back to the United States.

"I was English-speaking, but new to the United States," she recalled. "My parents put me in public school for kindergarten through sixth grade."

That school was excellent, with successful programs and a variety of extracurricular activities.

"I was in the gifted and talented program, and I was super challenged in elementary school," Jana said. "I have such vivid memories of art class and learning about impressionism in third grade. I can still remember all of the presidents in order because we learned it in school. There's just a lot that has stuck with me because school was fun and interesting. I loved elementary school."

Meanwhile, her parents saw to her spiritual development and encouraged learning in their home.

"During that whole time, I went to church, as well," she said. "My family didn't have a whole lot of money because we had been missionaries and were new to the United States, but I remember that we always had money for books. We might have only bought our clothes at thrift stores, but everyone was always reading and learning. I have very strong memories of reading with my family, and of that always being important."

But as the family situation changed, Jana's parents were mindful of the effect changes could have on their children, and planned strategically.

"When I was in sixth grade, my family moved to another city, and we rented an apartment while my parents looked for a house," she said. "For the purpose of not making me change schools later, they put me in a private Christian school, so that it didn't matter what neighborhood they moved into."

The change in schools did require some adjustment on her part.

"When I went to private school, in some subjects I was a little behind because the curriculum they used was very different from the one I had been exposed to," Jana said. "I remember my first day at that school, the teacher was diagramming a sentence, and I had never seen that before. I sat in that class and just cried because I felt so stupid, even though I had never been taught that, and it wasn't important in my public school.

"I found a lot of those kinds of things at the Christian school. I hadn't learned all of the Bible stories. I felt kind of dumb, so that was hard for me."

Jana faced some social challenges there, as well.

"The private school also had wealthier kids, who were dressed better and looked better," she said. "It was a very different environment from what my public school had been. At my public school, I was a bit of a tomboy and didn't shave my legs, and it was all good. But once I went to private school, it was all about how you looked and how you dressed.

"We didn't have uniforms, but we had dress code, so there still was that competition for how you dress. Junior high was hard for me both socially and school-wise."

Jana attended the only public high school in her small town, which was so small that there was no other choice available.

"I loved it," she said. "I was super involved."

Jana played sports, was part of student council all four years, and took all the advanced placement courses, where she was challenged by her teachers and coaches.

"I always felt like I had the resources at public school," she said. "Even when I was going through some hard times, I could talk to the counselor there. She and the teachers were always available to me.

"The whole city revolved around the high school, and I enjoyed that. You know everyone, and everyone knows you. I think it was a good environment for me," Jana said, "but that made moving to Los Angeles for college a little harder, even though I went to a small private Christian college."

For Jana, neither public school nor private school was the source of her spiritual growth.

"Growing up, I always felt my spiritual education was fostered by church programs that I was part of," she said. "I always went to Vacation Bible School and church camp, and we had good Sunday morning programs.

"But I also saw my parents reading the Bible, going to Bible studies, and having people over to do Bible study. My parents always modeled what it means to study God's Word and how to live it out."

Her school years were not without spiritual challenges, though.

"I was sometimes pressured to not follow Christian standards at public high school," Jana recalled, "but I think you have to eventually face that. With those pressures, you decide what you want to do.

"There was a period of probably a year where I made the choice to do what I wanted to do, rather than necessarily what God would want me to do, but I feel like that was part of my growing up. You have to face those pressures and make your own decision."

Jana saw her friends work through the same challenges.

"In my experience, everyone is going to face those at one time or another," she said. "Many of my friends who were more sheltered in high school then faced it in college, where you have more freedom and more opportunity to really screw up your life. Not that you have to totally mess up everything, but I think the temptations that I faced in high school were at an appropriate level. I knew what was right and wrong."

Her parents played a key role in coaching Jana through those years.

"I remember the summer between eighth grade and my freshman year, when I was getting ready to go to public school," she said. "My best friend started having sex with her boyfriend. We were 13, and I was mortified because I hadn't even kissed a boy.

"I talked to my mom. She said that some of my friends were going to make bad decisions in high school. I didn't need to do what they did, but to keep loving them and being their friend.

"That was important for me as a pastor's daughter. There were a lot of other PKs [preacher's kids] that I grew up with, and I saw more than one of them swing to the other end of the pendulum and go a little crazy.

"But I kind of had the fear of my parents and the fear of God, so I was a good girl. But the public school experience was important for me," Jana said.

"I think my parents prepared me well for high school," she said. "I had a pretty involved youth pastor's wife who was always available for me to talk with. And my sister, who is seven years older than me, was great to talk to, as well.

"Academically, the expectation was high," she continued. "My parents put it on me, but I was also driven, myself. I think academically I struggled with perfectionism, and was 'type A' about it, almost to a fault. I could have been more well-rounded.

"Both of my parents went to college, and my dad went to graduate school. I always knew that I would go to college and to work someday because both of my parents worked."

Today, Jana works as a nurse in a major hospital system and volunteers with her husband as part of the house church where they are active in various community ministries. As they consider a time ahead when they might become parents, Jana has drawn some thoughtful conclusions about what she might want for her own children.

"When it comes to schools, we will look for one that is strong in not only academics, but will also consider what kind of activities and programs they have, like theatre or art in addition to athletics," she said. "I locked into academics, when I actually have other talents that went untapped for a long time, so a well-rounded school is important. To me, as long as a specific public school can maintain values and a high education level, that's great."

As she considers helping children develop relationships with Christ, she particularly wants to avoid a mistake she has seen some Christian parents make.

"I've seen a number of our friends who grew up in church with us who are now no longer in church," Jana said. "Their parents act toward them like they want them to be 'Christian' more than they want them to be part of their family, leaving them with the feeling that they are not valued because they don't mirror the parents' beliefs.

"If a child doesn't feel they have a choice with it, then it often doesn't become authentic, and they never develop their own relationship born of personal belief."

Jana hopes to encourage her children, and lead by example, without making assumptions or demands.

"I want to do what seems best for my kids, and to love them as they are. I don't think we get to write our children's stories, but we need to trust God that he will work everything out," she said.

Study the Example: *Sandra*

Sandra's words of insight and advice for parents have the weight of valuable experience: from being a housewife homeschooling her four children through getting an education degree and teaching, then supervising two private Christian schools through their first accreditation process and serving as the principal of a private Christian school, to working for the past twelve years with a state education service agency that assists public schools.

As a parent, she has had her own kids at various times homeschooled with her, in private Christian school, and in public school, so we get the benefit of her viewpoints that are both parental and professional. In the words of your high schoolers: winning!

"I began homeschooling because our family had several moves scheduled over upcoming years, and I didn't want my kids to have to keep changing schools," Sandra said. "Then we settled in a big city, and because I was from a small town in the Midwest, what I heard on the news made me afraid of public schools.

"But my husband's job situation changed, and I needed to work. I decided that if I had to work, I wanted to take my kids with me, so I looked for teaching jobs at Christian schools," she said.

She was hired to work as a receptionist at a Christian school, which allowed her to complete the last few hours she needed for her education degree, but her main responsibility was to coordinate all that was needed for the school to become accredited.

"Working with the accreditation team from the Association of Christian Schools International, I learned about what great Christian schools should look like," Sandra said. "They have to follow all of the requirements of public schools as far as having scope and sequence defined in curriculum, with clear learning objectives. They have to ensure that there is spiraling curriculum, which defines what is appropriate for students to learn in each subject at every grade level, to prepare them to move on to the next, and the next, and the next.

"It was a long process, to prove that the school does all of that. Schools must do an extensive self-study, and then ACSI sends a team to evaluate whether or not the school has correctly implemented everything," she said.

Because of her experience with that process, another Christian school then hired Sandra as principal, with the goal of having her guide them through becoming accredited, as well. Again, her children would attend school where she worked, with one exception.

"My oldest was a junior, and because the school wasn't accredited yet, I didn't want to risk her high school credits being accepted, so she went to public school," Sandra said. "She was happy and successful there, and graduated high in her class. Our only disappointment was that because she had not started there as a freshman, to work her way up through the organization, she wasn't allowed to even try out for the varsity dance team, even though she had been dancing her whole life.

"Later, my youngest son begged us to let him attend the public high school, so for his junior year, we let him," she said. "Christian school was not necessarily the best fit for him, as he was a struggling learner. I realized in hindsight that I had been too narrow in my thinking for him. If he had been in public school all along, he would have had diagnostics done, and would have been helped from a much earlier point. I should have had him tested on my own much sooner. But instead, because he felt like 'odd man out' in his private school classes, he began to say, 'I don't fit here,' and he started to withdraw. I see now that was his cry for help."

Her son attended the public high school for his junior year, but when he had trouble passing the required state achievement test, which could threaten his graduation, he went back to the Christian school for his senior year.

"He was a good athlete," Sandra said, "and he played basketball every year except his junior year, which was a positive for him. But again, because he had not been at the public high school all along, he could only play junior varsity sports at the public high school, when he would have easily made varsity otherwise."

Sandra sees many strengths that would recommend private Christian schools.

"If your faith is aligned with the tenets of the Christian school, then the things you want to instill in your children will be reiterated at school, in terms of character and the principles you want them to live by," she said. "Also, in a private school, there is more opportunity to take action when behaviors fall outside of those principles. Students can be expelled for specific violations, and students and families know that up front.

"The smaller environment allows for a tight sense of community, as you are seeing the same families during the school week, and often at church on weekends. Parents can know the families of their kids' friends more deeply, and know who they can trust to allow their children to go to others' houses, so there's a positive social impact," she said.

"Because often one family will have siblings spread across elementary, middle school, and high school, the relationship that the school staff builds with a family allows parents the opportunity for significant input, and parents are asked to be part of more events," Sandra said, "and because of smaller class sizes, parents can depend on the teacher to be in tune with the needs of each child, and even help the teacher in the next grade level to understand that child early in the next year."

There are, however, possible inherent weaknesses to consider in many private Christian schools, too.

"Private schools must depend on tuition, which impacts teacher earnings," Sandra said. "That makes it harder to attract the best teacher talent. So you tend to get more older, retired teachers who are devout Christians but not dependent on salaries for a living, and it is difficult to balance that with younger, perhaps more vibrant, teachers because they are still dependent on salary for living expenses.

"Many Christian schools find that they don't have as much money to spend on professional development for faculty, and the same lack of funds can result in a lack of support for both special needs students and those who are on the high end of achievement, so they tend to be more focused on the needs of the average student," she said.

"The smaller number of faculty members limits elective choices, due not only to numbers of people but also to which areas teachers might have expertise that would qualify them," Sandra said. "The same concerns would limit the number of programs a school could offer, too. For example, a school might not be able to field both a soccer team and a baseball team, because there is just not enough money, or because there are not enough kids."

But there are ways that parents can fill in for some of the gaps.

"Parents would need to find things like club ball for their athletes or places for their kids to pursue art or music lessons, for example," Sandra said.

She believes there are both advantages and drawbacks to weigh in public schools, as well.

"Although you hear a lot of negative talk about testing in public schools, I actually think that can be an advantage because it gives teachers data and helps them see the gaps in a child's learning," she said. "By using a baseline of what all kids should learn, we can identify when a student has not learned. Of course, the drawback is that it can cause educators to limit students to working on only what is required. But the funding that is there allows for great support for kids who are struggling, providing people who are specifically trained to help."

The effectiveness of public schools will vary.

"It all comes back to the leader," Sandra said, "and how that person does at engaging and inspiring the teachers. Considering the large numbers of students that go through the system each year, many of our public schools do an amazing job."

On the downside, she thinks that a child from a Christian family has the potential to feel socially isolated.

"Because parents are not necessarily making strong social connections with a classmate's whole family," Sandra said, "there is the tendency to limit our child's social interaction. It's sometimes hard for parents to be comfortable with the idea that their child can have strong friendships that parents don't completely understand."

In the upper grades, because there are so many students competing for things like positions on varsity teams or head cheerleader or club president or yearbook editor, a student has to hone in on one or two activities, so there is less variety of experience available.

"There's more pressure and competition for the things that make for a well-rounded child, and it can result in a student deciding, 'I'm not good enough.' Kids can become discouraged, especially if their parents don't have the ability to provide outside experiences, like CYO or YMCA sports, and so on," Sandra said.

She believes it is important for parents whose children are in public school to make it a point to be involved and active in the community.

"The schools always need volunteers," she said. "You don't necessarily have to do the big, time-consuming things, either. Volunteer to help one teacher, or look for a way to help another family. Don't be afraid for your children to be around kids you don't know, but instead, reach out and get to know the other families in the school community.

"I know that's hard when you are a working parent," she said, "but just ask yourself, 'What is one thing that I can do?'"

Overall, Sandra says her best advice when making the decision is to consider the whole child.

"We have to recognize that our children are all individual, with individual needs," she said. "Don't be afraid to make a different decision for each different child.

"Sometimes Christian parents hesitate to send their kids to public school because they worry that they will fall in with the wrong crowd. The one thing I knew about my daughter is that that wouldn't happen, and it didn't.

"The thing I feared with my son is that it would happen, and it did. He was running with the wrong kids, but then they were also going to church with him on Wednesday nights," she said. "If the only reason you are sending your kids to Christian school is to keep them away from bad things, then you are going to be disappointed, because all of those things happen at Christian schools, too. The only difference is that administrators at Christian schools have more decisive ways to deal with it."

Sandra added a tip for parents when troubles do come up.

"Don't always believe your kids' stories as a parent, no matter where they are going to school," she advised. "If you can't hold the belief that every teacher intends to do right, then you are in the wrong place.

"If your child tells you about something that happened in math class, first go to that math teacher, and give him or her the opportunity to give you their assessment of the situation. If that does not resolve the issue, then go to the principal, but it is much more effective and better for your children if you go to the teacher first."

Looking back over her career in education and her experiences as a Christ-follower desiring to raise her children to know and love God, Sandra has drawn some conclusions that are a bit different from what she believed in the beginning.

"So many times as Christians, our way of trying to understand what God wants from us is to come up with a new set of rules," she mused. "But Jesus didn't say he came to give us more rules. He says he came to give us abundant life. I was just re-reading the book of Romans, where it says that what we do to prove our own righteousness is really like filthy rags. I knew that, and believed in God's mercy for myself, but I had unintentionally put a performance mind-set on my kids.

"Having their mom be principal of a Christian school was a lot like being preacher's kids for them. I put a lot of pressure on them to behave," she said. "Now, I think that instead I would ask more questions, like 'What's really going on?' and 'What are you thinking and feeling?'"

After her years of being in lots of different public schools, working with teachers and administrators there, Sandra has a last bit of insight to share with parents considering the best fit for their children.

"I've discovered that there's lots of 'covert' Christianity in public schools," she said. "There are many, many educators who are teaching God's Word every single day, without telling the students specifically that it is God's Word. They are focused on loving and supporting their students every bit as much as those who teach in Christian schools.

"The whole thing about Christianity is that there's a way we are supposed to deal with people," Sandra said. "Whether we choose a fishbowl, where we are with the same people over and over, or we decide to swim in the whole ocean every day, either way, we are supposed to be salt and light to those outside the fishbowl.

"Too many Christians walk in fear, and that is not what God intends for us to do," she said. "Whatever decision you may make for your kids, God wants us to walk in faith!"

Study the Example: *Holly*

Leaving her coffee untouched for the moment, Holly leaned across the table and began our interview with a strong statement that would set the tone for our whole conversation.

"Whether we talk about me as I was growing up, about my students over the years, or about my own children, there is one key," she said. "Learning has to be enriched at home."

Growing up in a Christian family, she attended her church preschool and kindergarten, but went to public school from first grade through her graduation from high school. She chose to get her degree in education from a Christian university, working part of that time as a nanny for a family who homeschooled their daughter. Over her thirteen-year career, she has taught elementary grades in a private school, and various grades and subjects in both public middle schools and high schools in two different states. Today she teaches at the same low-income public high school that she attended, and she and her husband, who is a minister, have their son attending their public elementary school, where they are leaders in the PTA.

"Schools offer general knowledge about every subject," Holly said, "but it is up to parents to give their kids the richer experiences that bring learning to life.

"In elementary school, for some reason, I found World War II interesting. My parents bought me the American Girl book about Molly, a little girl growing up at that time. They took me to a World War II museum, and just generally fed my interest with whatever they could find," she said. "There's no way any school could cater to every child's interests.

"Even parents who are homeschooling have to be sure that they aren't just doing the prescribed curriculum. You have to ask your children what they are interested in, and look for that thing that puts a spark in their eye. We have to actively search for other ways than just worksheets to educate our children," Holly said.

As busy as she is with teaching, that's something that she and her husband try to do as a matter of course with their own child.

"When our son showed an interest in planets and stars, we made it a point to look for documentaries about astronomy and space that we could watch together, and we made a weekend trip to Houston, so that we could tour NASA with him," she said. "But there's lots you can do that's free, too. He loved it when we just used a flashlight and a couple of balls in his dark bedroom to demonstrate how the moon and earth orbited. With everything that's available on the Internet now, there's really no excuse for not being involved with our kids' learning. For example, YouTube has a ton of videos of cool science experiments to do with kids."

But making those connections takes making an intentional effort.

"We have to be talking to our kids all the time about school, so that we know what is capturing their attention," Holly said. "But in turn, we should be asking, 'What is hard for you right now?' too. My son is having a challenge right now with counting money, so every time we're in the store, I hand him money, and he counts it for me. That's not a big thing, but it's helping him practice, and see what he's learning at school in the context of everyday skills."

Holly's approach carries over into spiritual instruction, too.

"For me, there's not much difference, as far as a parent's job," she said. "We should be enriching all areas, spiritually, too. Of course, if our kids are in public school study of the Word, and our family's faith becomes like an extra course at home. But we still customize their enrichment in that, too.

"I could have read every book there was on World War II, but no teacher was going to be able to tell me about how my grandfather became a decorated war hero. Only my parents could do that. It's the same thing when you talk about your faith. No amount of private school Bible class was going to teach me about how my great-grandparents survived the Depression and tell me the stories about how God provided for them when there seemed to be no hope. Those stories are part of the foundation of my faith in tough times as an adult, and that had to come from home," Holly said. "It's about what you model, about your conversations, and about the time that you spend together."

Elementary school was a good time of learning and making friends for Holly, who brought from home every day the idea that she was there to look out for those who needed her friendship and her prayers. She recalls one vivid memory, from the early days of the See You at the Pole nationwide event.

"I was the only student standing at the flagpole at my elementary school that morning," she recalled. "When the custodian came out to raise the flag, he asked me what I was doing there. I remember telling him, 'I'm praying for the school and the teachers and the kids and their families.' And he smiled and said, 'Well, then I'll pray with you,' and we stood there and prayed."

But when she moved to middle school, it was an extremely negative environment. Kids were routinely bullied, and she often found herself eating alone. As they became aware of the situation, her parents began attempting to work with the school administrators and faculty, but with no real results.

"If it hadn't been for the fact that they were building a new middle school that I would go to the following year, my parents would have moved me to private school," Holly said. "But the new school was wonderful, with a positive, encouraging faculty and administration, and I made good friends and really thrived there.

"Parents just have to know that they can't be so set on one way. You have to be ready to be flexible because a school can change overnight, depending on the people in charge," she said. "And it depends on the individual child, too. I liked having the opportunity to defend my faith and to share it. I had support at Sunday school and youth group, and at home, and I liked the challenge of finding other friends who loved God, but I was a natural leader.

"A child doesn't have to be a leader to be successful in school though," Holly said. "You just have to pay close attention to who is leading, if your child is easily influenced. Have a lot of pretend conversations, where you talk through a possible scenario, and ask your child, 'What would you do?'"

And the truth is, there are bullies and kids who do inappropriate things everywhere. Holly recalls one of her major challenges teaching a fifth grade class at the Christian school.

"I had six girls in my class who had grown up going to church and the school together," she said, "and suddenly that year, two of them developed 'mean girl' complex. Three of the others followed whatever those two said, and then there was the one who was the target. I tried everything, even making them miss recess to do devotions. They were as bad as anything I had to deal with as a student or a teacher in public fifth grade, and they were all from Christian families. Everything eventually worked out great, and all six are lovely young women today, but that was a bad year. My point is that private school is not necessarily all that different from public school, because in both places you are learning to deal with people."

The student population of the public high school that Holly attended included a wide cross section ethnically, culturally, and economically, which meant that she had to learn to deal with some people in situations outside of her norm.

"I remember sitting in choir in ninth grade, and this girl got up and walked across the room to me, and said, 'I want to fight you.'"

"I was shocked, and I said, 'Me? Why?'"

"'You smile too much,' she said. 'You act way too happy.'"

"I said, 'I'm not gonna fight you,' and she said, 'Yes, you are,' and I kept saying, 'I'm not going to, I'm not going to,' over and over, until the teacher came over and defused the situation," Holly said. "We never did fight, and by our senior year, we were buddies in choir. As we were leaving school for the last time, she rolled down her car window and yelled, 'Have a great time in college!'"

Now a teacher at her old high school, Holly tells that story to her classes every year. But this year, a student raised her hand, and said, "Miss, I think that may have been my mom!"

Holly reached for her yearbook, and said, "Show me your mom's picture."

Sure enough, she turned right to the photo of that girl.

"Wow! That is her," Holly told her student.

"Yeah," her student said. "That was the year she was being abused."

That was something Holly had never been aware of, but she says that from now on, that will be part of that story when she shares it, to help her students learn that they don't always know what is motivating the people they meet.

A similar interaction with another student in choir had a permanent impact on Holly, too.

Her place on the practice risers was next to a boy named Jamie, who was a known gang member.

"A couple of times a week, he would ask me, 'How come you're always happy?'" Holly said. "I knew I should really lay it out for him, but I was a little intimidated by knowing he was in a gang, so I would just say, 'Oh, my faith . . .' and kind of trail off, even though it bothered me that I didn't have the guts to just tell him.

"Then, the summer before our senior year, a friend called me, and said, 'Did you hear? Jamie was killed in a car accident, and his mother wants us to sing at his funeral.' I spent the whole week just grieving, 'I should have said more, and now it's too late!'

"But at his funeral, after we had sung, the minister said, 'You all need to know that Jamie is in heaven today. Just two weeks ago, he stopped by the church to see me, and that day he prayed and asked Jesus into his heart.'

"And in that moment, I determined once and for all, 'I'm never going to let fear get in the way of telling someone about Jesus again,'" she said.

"For the most part, though, I found really good friends at school, mostly through the honors classes and the different activities I was in," Holly said. "I would tell parents, no matter what kind of school your kids go to, encourage them to participate in lots of things to ensure that they won't become drifters.

Another thing Holly urges parents to do is not only support and attend school activities but also open your house as the place where kids can hang out.

"I think that when kids of the opposite sex see your kids in your house, with your family, they understand how valuable your kids are. I believe that the boys at my school always treated me well because they saw how I was treated by my dad and my brother," she said.

"Because my friends in different activities had been to my house, and felt welcomed by my parents, they respected me, and they held me to being who I was," Holly said. "Even if they were drinking, if I had tried to, they would have called me out.

"But I never felt the pressure to, anyway. My parents had talked with me about what to do if I got somewhere and illegal things were going on. They told me I could always make them out to be the bad guys, but they also gave me a strategy that was pure genius," she said. "The minute I saw that there was alcohol, I would just say, 'Well, I have to go because I have another party to get to. I just wanted to come say hi to you guys, too,' and then I left. It worked every time!"

So, looking back, Holly is glad for several reasons that she attended public schools.

"I had lots more opportunities than I would have in private school because there were so many more courses available," she said. "I had so many wonderful teachers, and found precious Christian friends there. I can't imagine what my life would have been like if we had not been able to encourage and support each other. I had one teacher who let me know that she was praying for me at school every day. To this day, nearly twenty years later, though she has retired, she sometimes subs, and when I see her, she always lets me know that she still prays for me.

"And finally, I had to learn early to own my faith. From that first See You at the Pole, through leading the high school Bible club, I had to decide and choose to commit for myself. I wouldn't take anything for that," Holly said.

She has similar reasons for choosing to send her son to public school, as well.

"First, I really like what a school is in a community," she said. "Just last year, my son had to be in the hospital for a week, and the principal, the school nurse, and his teacher all took time from their spring break to come and visit him. A little girl in his class knew he liked dinosaurs, and she likes glitter, so she sent him a dinosaur that she had covered in glitter.

"The broader the circle of adults who care about our kids, the better. Even if our church had a school, I would still want him to have even more than his church family who love and care for him," Holly said.

"And most of all, I want him to own his faith," she said.

So, based on her own experiences in school, and on the wisdom gained from teaching in classrooms in both public and private school, if a friend asks for her advice in choosing how to educate their children, she has an answer ready.

"First, I would urge them to be very active. Go to the public school, and talk to the principal. Look into classrooms, the hall and the cafeteria. Notice how the teachers are working with students, and how both adults and kids are treating each other. Then, do the exact same thing for each of your other top choices," she said. "And most importantly, be flexible, and pray!

DO YOUR HOMEWORK

Your kids can thrive in public school, but they're going to need you every step of the way, from the first day that you smile and wave them into that pre-K classroom and go make your Panera scone soggy with your tears, straight through to the moment you nudge your spouse to get the camera ready because they've finally gotten to the P's at graduation. (Assuming your name is Perez or Peterson or Puggle . . . you know.)

There will be two important aspects of this assignment.

One is academic and involves what I like to call the "kitchen table curriculum," which is where I got the name for my website. This is *not* about breathing down their necks while they do homework, nor is it about doing their science fair projects for them, however much you may be longing to apply your mad scrapbooking skills to their display boards.

This is more about extending their interests, helping them exercise their own particular intelligences, and most of all, connecting their learning at school to the biblical, spiritual aspect of life.

You get to be the one who inspires and guides them into the wonders of learning! And *you* get to be the one who guides them into developing a worldview that sees the hand of God, and a heart that responds to every need of his children.

Before you allow self-doubt to butt in here, understand that this doesn't require a degree in education or three years at seminary. All you need is an understanding of your child's strengths and weaknesses, and the willingness to create some shared experiences that relate to what they're doing in class at the time.

Even before they start school, you want to read to them. Get them in your lap or sit close together, and look at books. Examine and talk about the pictures, identifying letters and colors and numbers. When you're out and about, make it a game to find the same things in your surroundings.

If your child learns by touching, take a second with some Play-Doh to help him form some letters or numbers. If music seems to be her thing, sing the alphabet song together, touching the letters on a page as you go.

No need to make it last long, or to force the issue. If you're having fun with it, they will, too.

The summer that my daughter was three, and she had the attention span to handle it, I read one chapter from the Chronicles of Narnia aloud to her each afternoon before her nap, doing my best to give the characters voices. Before we were through the first book, she was pointing to words on the page and asking me, "What is that word?" The added bonus was that she came to love the series as much as I do, and we still share our love of all things Narnian today. I did the same with my son, who made it a point to text me photos of the famous wardrobe when he visited the C. S. Lewis museum on a recent trip to Chicago.

It's simple things, like working together to double a favorite recipe to practice multiplication of fractions, or giving your child a collection of various coins and bills and letting them make a purchase of their choice at the dollar store to help with money-counting skills.

It is my personal belief that all science stands up to Scripture, so when there's a lesson that causes your child to bring home questions, get to the computer together, find all you can about the scientific research, and then search the Bible and trusted commentaries to see how they compare. It has been my experience that, if you are willing to dig a little, you will find harmony there.

As your kids study history, talk about the motives of the people in that situation, and imagine what God was asking of his followers at that time.

When you find a topic that sparks a particular interest in one of your kids, run with it! Our son went through a period of strong interest in the Civil War, so we made it a point to visit the battleground at Vicksburg, and took the time to see a cool diorama that enacted one of the major battles as we passed through Chattanooga. That interest eventually led him to move on to considering the moral aspects of slavery and then, as a high school and college student, to studying the writings of Dr. Martin Luther King Jr. and the civil rights movement on his own. All of that led him to develop his own sense of social justice and of what attitudes and actions are required of him as a Christian adult.

On a trip to New York City, I took our then five-year-old daughter with me to see *Big River*, the musical version of *Huckleberry Finn*. That sparked her life-long love of theatre and led to her career as a high school drama teacher. But that meant that our whole family has attended more community theatre productions, outdoor musicals we would come across on summer vacation, and school plays than we can number. It also meant participating in spur-of-moment family productions for our own entertainment at home.

Another time, on a rainy Friday night, we gave the kids, both in elementary school, poster board to create a news set, and helped them comb through the newspaper and put together a script for a news broadcast, including sports, weather, and a movie review. We helped them dress up as anchors and then recorded their version of "The AMS Evening News." The added bonus was that we can still pull that puppy out for parental blackmail purposes as needed. Heh, heh.

When it comes to enriching their education, every experience we give our kids counts! Every trip, whether to the next town over or another country, broadens their frame of reference and opens their minds. In his book *The Innocents Abroad*, Mark Twain said it this way: "Travel is fatal to prejudice, bigotry, and narrow-mindedness, and many of our people need it sorely on these accounts. Broad, wholesome, charitable views of men and things cannot be acquired by vegetating in one little corner of the earth all one's lifetime."[1]

Become museum nerds, attend some of the wonderful programs offered at our national parks, keep up with events planned at your library, take in cultural celebrations, attend local concerts and plays. Don't be in such a hurry on road trips that you blow past monuments or historic markers, and occasionally explore the side roads. Keep up with movie reviews and websites that feature educational and family-friendly activities. Avoid the every-weekend rut of housework, yard work, and Little League or ballet, and spend the occasional Saturday, or whole weekend, on a family adventure that gives your kids great real-life connections to science or history or math or the arts!

As your kids do their daily homework, or as you explore the wider range of learning with them, avoid the urge to emphasize grades. Focus instead on always investing their best effort, and on the joy of seeking excellence in all they do. When they do present you with hurried, sloppy work, in a calm, matter-of-fact voice, simply ask, "Is this your very best work?" If they answer no, then ask, "What can we do to help you make it better?" That might mean an extra trip to the art supply or dollar store, or a shared research session at the computer, but as long as you can manage to leave the ownership of the project to your child (easier said than done for some of us!), you will have taught a life lesson more valuable than any point of curriculum the assignment was connected to. This might also be the perfect opportunity to explore together what the Bible says about the quality of effort and work God wants from his children.

A highlight of my memories of my father was the Saturday when he took me, as a second grader, to the library and signed me up for my own library card. He then guided me to the children's book area and helped me select and check out some books. To this day, I remember the smell of the library, the way the sun shone through the tall windows onto the polished tile floor, and the importance I felt as I held his hand and approached the checkout desk. From then until I was able to drive, three Saturday mornings a month, Daddy took me to the library. On the fourth Saturday, he took me downtown to the bookstore, where I used my allowance to eagerly purchase the next Nancy Drew book in the series, until I outgrew it. By the time I graduated and left home, I had read almost every work of fiction in our town's library. (Then, there's the devastation I felt as a college freshman to learn that the campus library had *no* fiction section, but that's a story for another day.)

Always remember that you set the tone and pace for your family by your attitude and participation in their learning, and if you will make the effort, it is your input and guidance that will have the greatest impact on the life of your child.

Extra Credit: ✓
Pulitzer, Socrates, and "Okay, I Guess"

"How was school today?"

"Fine."

Whether their kids are beginning kindergarten or senior year, most parents are eager to hear all about that first day, and all the days after it. Dying for details, we can be disappointed by the one-word answers, yet we don't want to drill the kids with annoy-ing, repeated questions.

Maybe it's time for one of my favorite lessons from my days as a journalism teacher—The Art of Asking Questions!

Rule number one: Never ask a question that can be answered simply "yes" or "no."

"Did you have a good day?" "Do you have homework?" "Did you find the $10,000 bill I tucked into your Frito bag?"

Rule number two: Questions that begin with "what," "who," or "how" require detailed answers. "What was the best part of your day?" "Who did you eat lunch with?" "How do you get to check out library books?"

Rule number three: Wait for the answer. Everyone needs a moment to think of what they want to say in response to a question.

Rule number four: After you get the initial answer, wait, expectantly, a little longer. Most people will need to fill the silence and will begin to add details, giving you the real answer to your question.

Rule number five: Look the person in the eye and respond with nods and smiles of understanding and affirmation as they answer. That inspires them to keep talking. The wonderful thing about interviewing our children is that the practice grows as they do. Interrogation, which none of us enjoy at any age, gives way to conversation, particularly valuable as they move from elemen-tary to pre-teen and teen years.

Instead of letting information about someone making poor choices and suffering consequences at school turn into a parental lecture, make it a teachable moment instead by asking questions.

"Why do you think she did that?" "What should he have done instead?" "How do you think you would handle the same situation?"

In education, we call that the Socratic method, and research shows it to be much more effective than lecture, as it leads the student to think and make conclusions that he will then own.

These conversations are especially effective as we lead our kids to develop compassion, courage, integrity, and wisdom that they can apply to situations they encounter every day.

So when you've made it through the brutal pick-up line traffic or on the way home from football practice or gymnastics, ask your children questions that would make Joseph Pulitzer and Socrates proud.

You'll be amazed at what your kids will tell you!

POP QUIZ

1. Does my child have learning styles or particular needs that can only be met in public school?

2. What, if any, are specific reasons why the public school my child would attend would be unable to provide the education and experience necessary to meet our family goals? Would we be able to fill in any gap at home?

OUTSIDE READING

This is an excellent post from the blog *The Art of the Simple*. The title is "The Public School Parent's Guide to Learning at Home," and that's exactly what it is!

theartofsimple.net/the-public-school-parents-guide
-to-learning-at-home/

How important is home and family to the learning process? MDRC, a noted think tank and research organization on educational matters, released this report.

www.mdrc.org/publication/impact-family-involvement
-education-children-ages-3-8

With a bit less clinical perspective, parenting.com arrived at very similar conclusions.

www.parenting.com/article/help-kids-with-homework

Another site, parents.com, agrees and gives some tips on the right way to help.

www.parents.com/kids/education/homework/how-to-help
-kids-with-homework-without-doing-it-for-them/

Sometimes it just gets down to this. The *New York Times* offers an entertaining take on "helping" with homework.

www.nytimes.com/2014/06/22/opinion/sunday
/helping-kids-with-homework.html?_r=0

Stuck on a math problem? Yeah, there's an app for that! The app is called Got It Study, and it can be downloaded from Google Play.

Science takes on a whole new perspective when you learn about the people who made it happen. This blog introduces science biographies that will make the subject matter come alive. They all include some hands-on experiments that you can do with your kids.

*www.kidsdiscover.com/teacherresources/5-beloved-science
-biographies-activities-go-along/?utm_source=FB&utm
_medium=Post&utm_campaign=Blo*

One of the most important results of your child's education is that they become thinkers. At readwritethink.org, teachers offer tips to parents about how they can enhance that part of the learning process.

*www.readwritethink.org/parent-afterschool-resources/tips
-howtos/encourage-higher-order-thinking-30624.html*

This checklist from scholastic.com provides some ideas and activities that will connect with specific learning styles and multiple intelligences.

*www.scholastic.com/teachers/article/clip-save-checklist
-learning-activities-connect-multiple-intelligences*

"4 Things Worse than Not Learning to Read in Kindergarten" is an entertaining article in *Huffington Post*. But the message about the priorities of parental support is essential to every family.

*www.huffingtonpost.com/gaye-groover-christmus/4-things
-worse-than-not-l_b_9985028.html*

Section 3
FILL IN THE BLANKS

You've worked your way through the matching and multiple choice parts of the test, where you could select what you thought made the most sense to you. Now, grab a pencil or open a spreadsheet, because in this last section, you're going to pull it all together and prayerfully see how you can apply it to your particular child and current situation.

As you fill in the blanks and work on the final exam, hopefully you'll discover that you've found the best answer and discerned God's guidance in solving the important question of how to educate your child.

Chapter Six

THERE *WILL* BE HOMEWORK!

I had spent nine years teaching high school, and at the same time, two as a youth pastor's wife, before my first child was born. That gave me plenty of time to figure out my "endgame" for parenting, and I have to tell you I went just as much on how I *didn't* want my kids to turn out as on how I hoped they *would* be as young adults! (Just to be honest here, as any teacher will tell you, my list of possible baby names on the *never* list, due to classroom history, was about as long as my list of possibilities!)

If you spent the money to purchase this book and are investing the time to read it, then my guess is that you are a parent who cares about two things: you want your child to receive the best education possible, and you want your child to embrace faith in Jesus.

We have to know our endgame in this endeavor, too.

You know how there are some memes that pop up in your feed, like, twenty million times over a few weeks? Funny or pithy enough that the first time you "liked" it, but every time you saw it, it lost a little more of its punch, until you wanted a "stop post-ing this, it's making me crazy" button, and then finally, you just zoomed past it because it had no effect at all? That's the kind of Christian that we don't want our kids to be.

Maybe you've come across the hilarious old movie *Multiplicity*, where Michael Keaton tries to get control of his busy life by clon-ing himself, but each new clone is a little weaker and a lot more ineffective than the one before. That is what we want to avoid.

It just doesn't work to try to recreate our own relationship and experiences with Christ in our children, any more than it works to force our kids into repeating any other details of our lives.

Just as with talents and interests, and later, careers, following Jesus must be each child's own personal choice, and that rela-tionship will unfold in its own unique and wonderful way. It's possible that it will look nothing like our own.

What we do have the privilege of doing, though, is being the ones who introduce our children to Jesus, and nurturing the relationship as it develops for each child.

If our DNA, our fingerprints, and each separate snowflake that falls are unique in all the world, what would make us think that anything about parenting our children would work by formula?

Even if the cars that drive themselves, now being tested in a few cities, become commonplace, or if we can fly across oceans in planes set on autopilot, we will *still* never get to "program" our parenting.

No matter which method of education you choose for your child, if you want him or her to be an adult who follows Christ and lives an effective, fulfilled life, you *will* have homework.

Every day. Every night. On weekends. 24/7. For at least two decades!

In previous chapters, we've explored the various choices, and for each, we've talked about bases we would need to cover at home to ensure balance and effectiveness. But this is the heart of what every parent must understand.

Even more than attending church services together on Sunday, as important as that might be, it is what happens at home—on Monday morning as everyone gets ready for the day, on Thursday night at the dinner table, on Saturday after the soccer game—that will be crucial.

What your kids see you do will have far more weight than anything that you might say. How they see their parents treating each other, and what they observe in your attitudes toward others and in your reactions to the inevitable bumps and bruises of life, will speak volumes to them of the true value of living a life centered on a relationship with Christ. They see your sincerity, they are moved by your service, and they are guided by your integrity.

What they hear you say to each other, what they hear you say to the lady at the fast food drive-through who got the order wrong, or about the person who cuts you off in traffic, or about the people at your office will have huge impact on their idea of what it is to follow Christ.

The things that you choose to do with them, the tone and purpose of the time you spend with them, all send the message of their own value, not only to you, but to the world, and to God. What you say to them about themselves, and about God's love for them, will be written in their hearts, and will influence every day of their lives on this earth.

This is not intended to be just a book about education, but instead a book about life, and preparing our kids to live joyfully and with great impact.

So we start by connecting every aspect of education, including spiritual development, with the abundant life they were made for.

The basis for this twenty-year homework assignment is found in Deuteronomy 6, as God prepares the children of Israel to take up the new, fulfilling lives he has planned for them in the promised land. This is how it reads in *The Message*:

> ⁵ Love GOD, your God, with your whole heart: love him with all that's in you, love him with all you've got!

> ⁶⁻⁹ Write these commandments that I've given you today on your hearts. Get them inside of you and then get them inside your children. Talk about them wherever you are, sitting at home or walking in the street; talk about them from the time you get up in the morning to when you fall into bed at night.

Here it is in just a few powerful words. The creator of the universe, our God and the Father of Jesus, is telling us exactly how he wants our homes to look. Help with homework doesn't get any better than that!

The first step, and one we can't possibly download from the Internet or borrow from someone else in class, is to love God wholeheartedly, and get his Word and his ways inside of ourselves. So, according to this, the place to start is with an honest "gut-check." Do we love God from our whole hearts, instead of giving lip-service simply to appease those around us? Are we committed to following Jesus at every level of our lives? Do we want to educate our children and bring them up in a certain way because of our love for Jesus and our desire to share his love with them, or simply because it's what others in our circle expect us to do?

The second part, and the assignment we are taking on here, is to win the hearts of our children to Jesus. The method this passage gives sounds supremely simple. Talk about the things of God wherever we are—at the breakfast table, in the car on the way to school, in the evening at dinner, sitting in the den after supper, as part of the bedtime ritual. All. The. Time.

But God is not telling us to be constantly preaching to (or at!) our children. He is telling us to "talk about" God and his ways. That implies a natural, two-way conversation that has a theme that flows through everyday life.

That may sound impossible to someone who didn't grow up in a home where talk of God and his role in the world and the lives of family members was a common occurrence, but with just a little courage and purposefulness, it can become the commonplace thread that winds through the days, tying the family together in love as the story of each child becomes woven into the tapestry of God's eternal plan.

The effort to expose them to authentic love for God, to encourage them in their faith, to support them in their search for truth, and to share the joy of having an intimate relationship with Jesus is really quite practical and down to earth.

When the children are little, we talk to them about God in the moments that come up.

"Look at how hard it is raining! That is the way that God gives the trees and flowers the food they need to grow."

"Wow, there's a rainbow! Remember what God promised Noah when he saw the rainbow?"

"You don't have to be afraid to go to sleep. The Bible says, 'I will lay down in peace and sleep, for you alone, Lord, keep me safe.'" (My paraphrase of Psalm 4:8)

It's about being alert to every possibility, and grabbing every opportunity to talk about God that opens up. When you allow the conversation to naturally include God, then the home described in Deuteronomy will naturally evolve.

When your kids begin to attend school, or group tutoring, or any other activities that take them away from you for a while early on, take the time to talk about what happened while they were there.

"Did Jackson refuse to share? How did that make you feel? Should you share with Jackson next time? What do you think Jesus wants you to do?"

"Miss Joanne said that you helped put away the toys today. When you are kind and helpful, that makes Jesus proud of you, and we are proud of you, too."

When the children are little, our talk should focus on who God is, who Jesus is, and how he loves them.

As they get older and begin to encounter pressures and uncertainties outside of the safe walls of home, the conversations will move more toward talking about what motivates others, about what God might be asking of the children in their relationships with others. It will probably also include searching for honest answers in the Bible for sincere questions that will naturally arise from interaction, from study, from current events, or just from their own curiosity.

It's okay to honestly not have an answer, even after searching. I remember lying in bed, as a sixth grader, trying to figure out how God is eternally existent. I understood how he created all that is, and I understood that eternity had no ending, but I just couldn't grasp how God could *be*, without a moment of beginning.

The mistake we want to avoid in our spiritual parenting is shutting down our child's curiosity and questions. God is not offended by sincere seekers. In Jeremiah 29:13–14, he tells us, "'If you look for me wholeheartedly, you will find me. I will be found by you,' says the LORD" (NLT).

When the kids hit puberty, it will be time to talk about their choices for how they will conduct their lives, and it will be important to focus, not so much on the rules and things not to do, as on how responding to being loved by God by loving others guides their choices.

When we encourage our kids to view all others as God sees them, it begins to make sense that going to a strip club dehumanizes the women there, or that having sex in order to keep a dating relationship going is more about controlling than loving, encouraging, inspiring, or protecting the other person. Those conversations as we sit at home or drive down the road become a source of Godly wisdom that our kids can draw on in future situations, and they create a relationship of openness and trust between parent and child.

As our kids move into their upper teens and prepare to leave our homes to go out on their own, then our conversations, as much as we feel the desire to tell them everything we want them to remember, need to include more questions for them, where we wait for their answers and really hear what they say. This is the time to ask them what God seems to be telling them about their role and place in the world, and to work with them to research and discover the best way to prepare.

And every day, at whatever age, our kids need to hear us pray, and to be invited to pray with us. Develop a pattern of responding to events in your family, in the neighborhood, and in the world, with simple and heartfelt prayer.

Let your kids hear you pray for them, for their friends, for the nation, for the world.

Just the other day, we had both grandsons in the car, and in the way that cedar pollen affects people in South Texas, all of us were coughing and sneezing and miserable, and both of their parents were at home suffering from the allergies, too. When the eight-year-old said, "G-Diddy, my head and throat really hurt," I started praying out loud, specifically naming each person in the family, and asking for healing and relief for each, with a little more about what each was needing to get done that week. It got sort of detailed (maybe even long?), but the boys were quiet, so I was, umm, thorough.

When I said "Amen," the two-and-a-half year-old piped up from the back seat, "That was a good one, G-Mommy."

Greg and I are still laughing about that, but in that spontaneous "walking in the way" moment, our grandsons had learned something about the role of prayer in our lives.

From the first night you bring those babies home from the hospital, sleep becomes a precious commodity, and remains so as you move from those nighttime feedings to waiting up to be sure that teenager's pickup truck makes it to your driveway. But if your family has trouble finding time every evening to spend together, then it would be worth it to get up a little bit earlier to ensure that they are getting what they need for the day.

Just as you make the effort to pack a lunch that contains something more nutritious than slices of processed cheese and rolls of corn syrup disguised as fruit, it is important to their spiritual growth and health that they can carry with them the knowledge that they have your attention and concern and prayers.

Because for our kids, the choice was public school, we knew we had to be careful and vigilant every day, so we got up early enough to sit at the table for a few minutes, and have prayer, and conversation about what God might have for us in the day ahead, and to help our kids see themselves as having a mission and a purpose to love the people they would encounter that day. We made sure to support them in that, by sponsoring (and feeding) Fellowship of Christian Athletes, by supporting anything that was needed by the church youth group, and by opening our home to our kids and their teammates, classmates, and friends any time.

By doing this, as we talked about the day's events and our kids' concerns in their own lives and the lives of their friends, and the prayers we shared, the model in Deuteronomy 6 became the natural atmosphere in our home.

Now, our children are educated, effective adults who share the journey of following Christ, devoted to loving God and loving people, each in their own way.

You know those teachers you had who assured you that the only way to pass was to do your homework? When it comes to raising our kids, they were right!

Study the Example: *Ginny and Clint*

When Clint and Ginny married, they had a ready-made family in the three children that Ginny had previously adopted from the foster system, and because of their own schooling, they were confident that the academy that their church operated was the perfect place for the kids to attend.

Clint had attended both public and Christian schools as a student, and he had watched his dad serve as president of the New York Association of Christian Schools. Ginny's entire education had been in Christian schools.

But perhaps because each of the three kids had come from the foster system with their own sets of adverse circumstances, and then had weathered the difficult divorce of their adoptive parents, things did not go as smoothly for their children as they had thought they would, based upon their own experiences growing up.

"When Lizzy, who had been abandoned at the age of eight, first came to me," Ginny said, "she really needed to spend as much time as possible with family. We put her into a Christian school very near my parents' house, so that she could be there before and after school each day.

"But when she was an adolescent, we moved to a new state, and it seemed like a no-brainer to enroll her in the school connected to our church. When the time came for her to attend high school, she enrolled in the public school in our neighborhood. But then, because of her talent and interest in vocal music, she earned the opportunity to attend a fine arts magnet school. However, some turmoil she experienced during those years led us to have her spend her senior year at our church academy," Ginny said. "She eventually gained her balance, and as an adult she is a wife and sweet mother to her own children."

Kyle's road has been more difficult.

He began by attending the church preschool and kindergarten and then went to public school for first grade. He went back to the church academy but then experienced problems after making bad decisions, which prompted Clint and Ginny to homeschool him for a year. He finished his last three years at the church academy but has continued to struggle into adulthood.

"When my dad was serving the state association of Christian schools, I saw that there were some kids that would fall through the cracks," Clint said, "and I think that's what happened with Kyle. That system let us down, but I think it is because we put too much trust in the school, instead of taking a more active role in his spiritual growth at home."

Janey attended the Christian school through elementary school but switched to public school at the beginning of middle school. She was successful through her high school years, and as a college graduate pursues her chosen career.

Meanwhile, Ginny and Clint added two children of their own to their family.

Ashley and Emmy attended the church academy for their groundwork, but when Ashley was ready for second grade and Emmy had completed kindergarten, their parents decided to enroll them in the neighborhood public school.

"About the time Kyle graduated, we pulled the girls out of the church school," Clint said. "We were surprised to find that they had so many Christian teachers in the public school."

"It just happened that the public school in our neighborhood is a really good school, so that made it easy," Ginny said. "One of the teachers is married to a local pastor, and when we first visited, we noticed a flyer announcing a staff Bible study on the faculty bulletin board."

"We observed that there was a high ratio of parental involvement," Clint said. "The principal and teachers welcomed and encouraged parents. They even had an app to facilitate interaction between faculty and parents. We saw that the staff interaction with the kids in the halls and cafeteria was positive, all things that told us that this was a good school.

"Once we saw the struggles of our two oldest children, we knew we wanted Ash and Em to learn to survive in a world where they have to live out their Christianity, instead of just being good pretenders," he said. "Our son had learned to cover his tracks."

"I had to beg the church school administrators to punish him," Ginny said. "And even educationally, it turned out that he was not prepared for college at all. We were shocked to find, too, that our girls were behind when they went to the public school."

Meanwhile, Janey, who was expected to have learning issues because of her birth situation and prenatal exposure to drugs, thrived in public school.

"It has been so wonderful to see her learn and grow in that environment," Ginny said. "She has grown in her faith and as a person. Just recently, one of her friends all through school and college was baptized because of her influence through the years. It just shows that you have to decide on an individual basis what's right for your child."

Considering their experiences, the couple shared their evaluation of the strengths and weaknesses of each.

"I believe that in the church school, the good students excelled. Many of them went on to do well in top universities, and in their adult lives. But the ones who were not naturally good students were not necessarily assisted effectively," Ginny said.

Clint observed that one reason might be that church schools struggle with academics because of their financial challenge in hiring and retaining strong teachers and staff, whereas public school teachers must all meet standards.

"When administrators have to put faulty teachers into a faulty system, they are going to get a faulty product," he said.

"We can put our children into a Christian school, but it's no guarantee that Christ will get into them. It's almost like what they learn is to adopt the façade," Clint explained. "Instead of developing a personal relationship with Christ, some kids only learn to act as if they have that relationship, instead of learning to have genuine relationship every moment of every day.

"When Lizzy made the move to public high school," she told us, "It's a lot easier to spot the Christian kids in public school because they stand out. It was harder at the church school because they all looked the same."

"When we moved Lizzy and Kyle from Christian to public school, we thought that would fix it because there was no reason to be fake," Clint said, "but there was still the need for us to have been active regarding their spiritual lives at home.

"I spent some time as a coach at the Christian school, and many of those kids have gone on to become successful adults who follow Christ. Those that don't, I'm not so sure they had it when they were at the school. Christian schools are not bad. It's our assumptions as parents that is the weakness," he said.

Ginny believes the same is true about assumptions for parents who homeschool, as well.

"When we tried homeschooling, I am the one who failed," she said. "I realize now that my goal was not really to teach them. I was more into the idea of it, than the actuality. I liked ordering the books and setting up the folders, sort of thinking about how I was going to be the cute homeschool mom.

"But really I got into it because I was desperate, and I was using it as a form of punishment," she said.

"In the right setting, it can work," Clint said, "but as a form of punishment, that's not the right way.

"It also is not the guaranteed formula if your goal is only to protect your kids from the world. We know one family who homeschooled all nine of their kids for that reason, but today as adults, only one-third of those kids even have a relationship with their parents, much less a walk with the Lord," he said.

"I think homeschool didn't work for us because I didn't have the heart of a teacher," Ginny said. "I was a single mom, working from home, and really just trying to keep my son away from friends who were not good for him."

"But homeschool works if you want to be the ones to teach your kids how to live life in the world. Parents just need to remember that it is our responsibility to teach our kids how to survive, and live victoriously, in the world," Clint said. "Whatever way we choose, we can't give up and just let somebody else have that job."

For parents in the process of making the decision, Clint has some advice based on his and Ginny's experiences.

"It requires much prayer. It's as big as any decision in your life and theirs because you are preparing your child to live effectively long after you are gone," he said. "The only true right way is to make sure we are right with the Lord. Seeing us live out our relationship every day at home is the only way for our kids to catch it."

Extra Credit: ✓
Helping Your Kid Choose the Best College

If you wait until their senior year to start talking to your kids about college, it's game over before you even reach Labor Day! Especially since the deadline for early acceptance at most schools is in October. Wise parents begin the conversation years ahead.

1 Never pass any college or junior college without taking a quick drive through the campus, even when your kids are in elementary school!

> The more campuses they have seen, the broader their frame of reference will be. This will also plant the idea in their sweet little heads that they will be attending college someday.

2 Along with the architecture and the landscaping, notice the people and the atmosphere.

> Ask the kids, "What do you think it would be like to go here?"
>
> When my daughter was in middle school, I took her with me to a contest my students were in at the University of Texas. The two of us were in the van, circling to pick up the kids, when classes changed, and we were stopped at an intersection while college students crossed with the light. A school as large as UT will

obviously have an extremely diverse population, and sure enough, one of the boys who passed in front of our van was decked out in full Satanic robes, sporting a backpack he had covered with pentagrams. She looked over at me, her eyes wide and her mouth slightly ajar, and exclaimed, "I will *not* go to college here!"

3 By the time your kids are in middle school, two other questions should be part of the conversation as you cruise a campus.

"Does this school have programs that match your interests and goals?"

Our daughter went through a time when she thought it would be cool to attend Texas A&M. But when she discovered that they didn't offer a degree that would certify her to teach choir (her goal at the time), she focused her attention elsewhere. Every year that I taught, I would have students tell me that they wanted to major in journalism and planned to attend a local four-year university. I would need to point out to them that the school didn't offer such a degree, and indeed, didn't even have a student-produced newspaper or broadcast. However, the community college did have one of the nation's most highly regarded junior college journalism departments, with an automatic credit transfer to a university only a few miles away.

The other important question is "Can you see yourself here?"

No matter how much we may long for our kids to attend our own alma mater, this is a question that only they can answer, and until the answer is a resounding "Yes!" the search must continue. When your kids reach high school age, it's a really good practice for you to find a spot to have coffee or a soda, and let them walk the campus without you, especially if you can catch a time when classes are changing. That gives them an even better context for figuring out if they think they would fit in there.

4 Even though high schools don't usually give excused absences for college visits until the senior year, it is very important to make those official visits in the junior year.

When you are planning the visit, be sure to call ahead and set appointments with the dean of admissions, the financial aid office, and the head of the department for your student's intended major. Go prepared with every question you can think of. Sometimes you can even schedule an opportunity for your student to sit in on a class in her academic major area.

But also make it a point to explore a little in an unofficial manner. Walk through the dorm, check out the dining hall, and get a feel for what it's really like.

Immediately after the visit, make time to debrief, sharing thoughts and impressions. Remember to include the financial situation in the discussion, and talk about the desirability of freedom from debt, if at all possible, when starting out in life.

Even if you think it's going to kill you, let your student take the lead in this discussion, and listen way more than you talk!

5 The final decision really must be your child's choice!

Hopefully you have taught your son or daughter how to prayerfully, thoughtfully make such decisions in life, and this is the time when you need to trust your child and trust God in your child! The freshman year in college is so challenging that 30 percent of freshmen nationwide drop out before the end of the year, or do not return for the second year. You don't want your child to blame the inevitable difficulties and challenges on the fact that you made the decision for them. Along those lines, this seems like a good place to mention that we've written a fun, easy-to-read handbook for college-bound seniors or those already in the throes of that first year, that you might want to put into your kids' hands! It's called *Schooled! Taming Your First Year of College*.

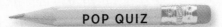

POP QUIZ

1. What are some things, either internal or external, that might hold me back when it comes to talking freely about God in front of my family?

2. When I honestly search my heart, how willing am I to allow my children to ask questions about God and their faith, and help them work to find the answers?

3. When I pray and think about a place to start that would work for our situation, what one first step comes to mind?

OUTSIDE READING

Discovering and defining who your family really is, is a vitally important component to every aspect of your family's life, including education. This site offers some thoughts regarding that.

www.familieswithpurpose.com/defining-family-identity/

From familyeducation.com, here are the reasons that family time is so important.

www.familyeducation.com/life/making-family-time/build -family-identity-through-family-time

When parent-child communication begins to break down, what can you do to restore and rebuild it? Here are some prompts that will always give you something to talk about with your kids.

www.focusonthefamily.com/parenting/building-relationships /celebrating-your-family-identity/family-talk-and-identity

Sometimes it's the simple things that build your family's identity. This article brings you back to the basics, pointing out the foundations that your family depends on.

www.thrivingfamily.com/Features/Magazine/2013/building -family-identity.aspx

My husband and I believe that family identity was so important in our home that we wrote two books about it. *Setting Up Stones* leads you in finding those priceless moments when you can create something meaningful and memorable for your whole family. In *The View through Your Window*, you can learn how to build a God-designed vision for your family.

Chapter Seven

ALL THINGS CONSIDERED

When it's time to make the final decision, expecting to find instructions written by an invisible hand on the dining room wall, like the one Daniel saw in the Old Testament, is probably a tiny bit extreme.

While he promises more than once in the Bible that he will guide our steps, and that he will answer when we ask, God also says he will give us wisdom, and that involves using the thinking and reasoning skills that he gave us.

So sincerely desiring God's guidance, it's now time to think through the details of the daily impact each choice might have on your family.

One Way or Another, This Is Gonna Cost Ya!

If you are wanting to homeschool, can you live on one income? Think through your monthly bills and expenses, your health coverage and costs, and the number and cost of vehicles you need. You might save money on things like school clothes or uniforms, lunches, and activity fees, but then you'll also need to factor in the cost of curriculum materials, co-op groups, and probably computer and Internet services. Remember, though, that your public library offers many of the resources you will need at no charge.

If private school is looking like your best option, then be certain that you can easily pay the tuition and any extra fees for field trips or participation in extracurricular activities. Will you need to pay for a band instrument or athletic gear like shoes with cleats? What will your kids require in the way of clothes, whether it is uniforms or meeting dress code? Find out what scholarships might be available and whether your family qualifies for any of them. Will you need to purchase textbooks and other instructional supplies, or are they provided? What will be the cost of lunches on a weekly or monthly basis?

Another, more subtle consideration is how much social pressure may be unintentionally placed on your child. If you are considering a private school where most of the families have a much higher standard of living than you can afford, will your child suffer adverse effects from not having the wardrobe, the acceptable brand of shoes, the computer, or the phone as the others, or of not being able to participate in certain activities with the others? In a perfect world, this shouldn't matter, but depending on the specific student community, it might. It is certainly something to be aware of, and prepared for, in making that choice.

While there is no upfront cost for public school, if you don't live within range of the district bus route, will you be able to afford the cost of transporting your kids to and from school each day? Again, estimate the cost of lunches, school clothes, and any fees or expenses for participating in sports or clubs. These are questions you can ask the counselor or coaches at the school, and they may vary from school to school, even within one district.

For example, students at some schools in my daughter's district are charged a costume fee for any drama productions they are in; whereas her department manages to costume shows from their budget. Pep squad and cheerleading teams usually have to pay for their own outfits, gym bags, and other spirit gear; whereas athlete's uniforms are provided. Some athletic teams provide shoes, while others do not.

And, unless you are homeschooling, remember that the school day probably will end before your work day does, so that means you will need to make arrangements for after-school care, and for the calendar days off that might not match your work schedule. Will you need to pay for a pick-up service that will take your kids to care, or will they be able to participate in an after-school program on their campus? It will be as important to research, and do on-site visits, to those programs as it is to carefully evaluate the schools you are considering. Or will a trusted neighbor or family member care for your kids in the afternoons? Will there be a cost involved for that? And remember to allow for some missed days of work if your kids are running fever or are otherwise too sick to attend school. Will that come out of your paycheck, or will it be covered?

Putting pencil to paper (old-school term . . . I'm sure there's an app for that!) can help you form a realistic picture of how your choice will affect family finances, and should be an important factor in making your decision.

Jammin' on Traffic

Along those same lines, parents need to think about the logistics that would be required on a daily basis, and how that would affect overall daily family life.

What time do classes begin and end? Are there transportation options, or will you need to drop off and pick up your kids?

What kind of commute, in how much traffic, will that involve? Does that work out with the requirements of your job? Will you need to plan for childcare early or after school, and can you afford that?

When our daughter and son-in-law were ready to become homeowners, they had no children yet. They bought a lovely home within a manageable distance from each of their jobs. But as days and years go by, things often change. They each took much better jobs, but those jobs added twenty to thirty minutes to the commute for both of them. Then, they became parents, and some unforeseen health issues for the baby meant that they would need us to care for him. But because we lived on the opposite side of the city, they suddenly found themselves spending an hour or more in the car both morning and evening, which cut into the time they had to spend together each day, and incidentally added to stress levels as they contended with traffic.

As happy as they were with their house, they realized that the location was impacting too many aspects of their lives, so they put it on the market.

Today they live only a few minutes from childcare (that would be my husband and me!), and less than fifteen minutes from their jobs. That change made a huge positive difference in how the days go for their entire family.

More Details!

Every family and every kid in that family is different, so here's a list of questions to ask that may or may not apply to your crew. But if you see yourself in one of these, then now is a good time to figure out your answer to that, too.

How does the school you are considering handle behavior problems and discipline? Do you approve of this method, both for your kids and others in their classes?

What is the attendance policy? Will your family be able to follow it?

For instance, we had neighbors who decided to homeschool their children one year because the dad's job was going to require extensive travel for that period of time. They purchased an RV and saw the country from one end to the other, enjoying an extended family field trip in American history and geography as they went.

I had a student whose grandmother required an injection every morning, and because of the hours and requirements of his parents' jobs, he was the only one in the family who could administer it. But that meant that he was late to first period every single day. When he told me why he was consistently tardy to my first period class, we made special arrangements with counselors and administrators for him to be able to do that without it counting against him.

Will your teen need to work and perhaps have a shortened school day?

There are schools that even offer programs where they help students find jobs, and students can earn academic credit for working half-days. There are also schools that will work with a student's schedule to allow them to leave campus early to report to a job.

If you know you have some special circumstances, ask questions, try to make arrangements, and factor that into your final decision.

What if your child has special health issues?

Investigate the services and situation at each school you are considering. Public schools have federal requirements for making individualized education plans (IEP, in teacher talk), but depending on the source of funding, private schools may not have to fulfill that requirement. And the way those plans are carried out from school to school can vary wildly.

We are blessed to have a dedicated, highly efficient, and caring school nurse at the public elementary school our grandson attends. Because he has cystic fibrosis, he must see her several times a day for his medication, and his parents must rely on her to alert them when there is a spike in cases of respiratory illness among students so that they can keep him at home. Not only does she diligently fulfill those responsibilities but she is also a loving, encouraging adult in his life.

So whatever special circumstances you may have, from a child with asthma who may need to use her inhaler, to one who needs wheelchair access or other accommodations, knowing how your child will receive the attention and support she requires will be a huge factor in your decision.

If your child has a particular special interest, will the school address it?

If your eighth-grade son is six-foot-three, weighs 250 pounds, and loves football, you obviously don't want to send him to a high school that does not have a football team. (College scholarship money—I'm just going to leave those three words right here.)

If your child is fascinated by science or shows passionate interest in music, or dance, or acting, will the method of education you choose provide the support and training they need and desire? Or if not, will you be able to offer opportunities from another source?

Sometimes we recognize in a child such extraordinary talent and desire that it becomes the priority in providing their overall education. We have friends whose young daughter is so naturally talented and so highly motivated and driven to succeed in gymnastics that her parents have her at a gymnastics training facility that also provides schooling. The little girls attend classes and also train there every day. We are pretty sure we're going to see her in the Olympics in a few years.

If you have more than one child, and it is obvious that private school is perfect for one but public school is what the other needs, how will you handle it?

The timing of pick-up and drop-off, a school year calendar that may not match, one with a soccer game on the same day as the other's academic decathlon competition are all things that need to be hashed out as part of the decision process.

Overall, while it seems noble to sacrifice for our children to have the best that we can give them, the truth is that what is most important is a peaceful, stable home where they are valued, encouraged, and nurtured in their love for Jesus. A solid education is important, as it prepares them to effectively fulfill their purpose and calling, both as children and as adults. We miss the point if we put ourselves in a place where financial worries or time crunches create stress that will undoubtedly have a negative effect in our homes.

An honest evaluation of the practicality of choosing one school over the other may help you narrow the list of schools to consider, as you seek the best option for your family.

The individuals in our families and the circumstances in which we live are all a part of God's excellent, loving desire to bless and use us. As you work through the process, you can be confident that God is for you, and for your kids, and will certainly guide you to a place where he can give you his best blessings!

POP QUIZ

1. What amount of money can we truly afford to invest in education expenses for each child?

2. Are there some possibilities on the list of choices that we've been thinking of that we need to remove from consideration due to the realities of our finances at this time?

Chapter Eight

FINAL EXAM

So here you are, down to the night before the final exam.

You've read the chapters and answered the questions at the end of each.

You've done the outside reading (well, *most* of it), and you've made notes about your own ideas and reactions to all the material.

You've made some field trips, searched online, even talked to some people who took this course before you.

Now, I really don't want you to end up like my son's college roommate the night before a final at the end of the first semester of their freshman year. He was planning to stay up all night, cramming, and then go straight to the exam first thing the next morning. However, he fell asleep with his face on the open text, and when my son's alarm woke them the next morning, the exam had already been over for thirty minutes.

For some reason, maybe because I had taught his roommate in high school, they called me in their panic, fearing that Vic's academic career was over.

"Mom, what can he do?"

Because it just so happened that this was a scene from a recurring nightmare that began *my* freshman year in college, and continues to this day, I was ready.

"Look at the exam schedule, and see if the professor has another section of the same course, and go to that exam," I told them. "Explain what happened, and ask him to let you take it then. Play the innocent freshman card, and beg if you have to."

They checked the campus exam schedule and discovered that the professor was indeed giving the same exam again that afternoon, and it didn't conflict with any of Vic's other course exams. All he had to do was go and throw himself on the mercy of the professor.

I couldn't stand the suspense, so I called my son that night.

"What happened? Did Vic get to take the exam?" I asked.

"Uh, yeah," my son laughed. "It turns out he had read the schedule wrong to start with, and that *was* his scheduled exam!"

So to keep you from dealing with an unproductive cram session, I have created the ultimate final study guide in this last chapter. (As I teacher, I always rolled strong like that. You're welcome.)

By now, you probably have two, maybe even three, choices that you have narrowed it down to. So I suggest that you take each possibility, one at a time, and answer these ten questions. If you're a spreadsheet kind of person, sweet. If not, just lay your notes out side by side, and get a good look at how the choices seem to stack up against one another. You could even go so far as to weight the different questions according to their comparative value to your family, and add up total points at the end.

Ten Big Questions

1 What are the specific spiritual strengths and needs of my child at this time? What are the next steps in cultivating my

child's spiritual growth? How does it appear that growth might be affected by this choice?

2 Academically speaking, how will the particular learning style and intelligences of my child, and any specific educational needs, be met in this instructional setting?

3 Based on research into the curriculum, outcomes such as ratings and test scores, the campus visit, and interviews with administrators and/or other parents, what were the strengths and weaknesses of this particular school?

4 How will this particular choice affect the practicalities of family life from day to day? Specifics to consider are location and start/end times for the school, or how homeschooling will work as far as use of instructional time, and time for other necessities and activities.

5 What is the overall spiritual and social atmosphere we will be putting not only our child but our entire family into? Consider what we have observed about the interactions of administrators, faculty, other students, and the families in the school community. What do we see as the probable role of our child and our family there?

6 What extra things will we need to do to enrich our child's training spiritually, academically, socially, and in developing talents, gifts, and special interests? Will we be able to make the necessary investments of time, transportation, and general support?

7 How will this choice affect our plan for spiritual growth as a whole family? Do we need to be in a place where all of us are receiving extra learning, input, and encouragement spiritually? Or are we as a whole, and our child individually, strong

enough to consider this choice as a mission? Is it a mission we believe God is asking our family to fulfill?

8 If homeschooling is an option we are considering, how deeply can we commit to the time and effort required for doing the job well? What will we be able to provide in the way of the opportunity to develop relationships outside of the family? What resources are available, in the way of time and funds, to give our children outside instruction and experiences in advanced academics, fine arts, or athletics?

9 What will be the concrete bottom line on all expenses? Include possible loss of one income if homeschooling, or, in addition to private school tuition, the cost of uniforms, activity fees, and after-school care. Also add in cost of outside lessons and gear in music, dance, athletics, and so on. Remember things like extra gas and mileage if you would be taking your child to a school outside of your neighborhood. Even things like time crunches forcing you to eat out several times a week should be part of your financial evaluation.

10 Is the whole family in unity on this decision? Not only do both parents need to be in agreement and equally committed to making this choice work, but ideally your child should be positive about the decision, as well. One more time, as an entire family, go back over your "why" for education and your particular goals, and be certain that all the checkpoints align.

And finally, with all of your research and responses to these questions laid out before you, pray together, and ask God to give you his wisdom and direction as you come up with the very best decision you can make for your child and your family.

Hebrews 11:6 says, "Because anyone who wants to approach God must believe both that he exists *and* that he cares enough to respond to those who seek him" (*The Message*).

Trusting that God loves you and has only good in mind for you and your children, you can act in faith that he will honor your prayer and effort here, and that the decision that you come to will be pleasing to him.

And as your entire family sets out on your adventures of exploring the knowledge of God and his world together, I will be praying for you all, that like Jesus as a child, each of you will increase "in wisdom and stature, and in favor with God and men" (Luke 2:52 NKJV).

OUTSIDE READING

The United States Department of Education's "Four Steps to Selecting a School for Your Child," can be found at readingrockets .com. It's a thorough checklist that will lead parents toward making an informed decision.

www.readingrockets.org/article/four-steps-selecting-school -your-child

This booklet is a "must-have" for parents as they make their decision about their child's education. It's a great starting place because in it the Department of Education has covered all the basics. Start here and add some more specific information that will match your own needs and situations.

www2.ed.gov/parents/schools/find/choose/choosing.pdf

Before your child's education process begins, you can download this pre-K checklist from edutopia.com.

www.edutopia.org/resource/3-step-kindergarten-planning -checklist-document?col=482941%3Futm_source%3 Dfacebook&utm_medium=cpc

Here's some more kindergarten information from edutopia.com.

www.edutopia.org/article/search-for-perfect-kindergarten -nora-fleming?utm_source=facebook&utm_medium=cpc

www.edutopia.org/article/choosing-kindergarten-what-does -research-say-youki-terada?col=482941%3Futm_source%3 Dfacebook&utm_medium=cpc

The Paideia principles are an educational philosophy that establishes a foundation for what learning and school should be. You can use the principles, add some of you own, and develop your own philosophy that will serve to guide you in decisions throughout your child's education.

www.paideia.org/about-paideia/philosophy/

Notes

[1] "Louie Giglio Mashup of Stars and Whales Singing God's Praise," YouTube video, 14:06, posted by "socialpipeline," September 27, 2011, www.youtube.com/watch?v=7zWKm-LZWm4.

[2] Howard Gardner, *Frames of Mind: The Theory of Multiple Intelligences* (New York: Basic Books, 2011).

[3] Tim Lambert, phone interview with the author, February 28, 2017.

[4] Mark Twain, *The Innocents Abroad* (Oxford, UK: John Beaufoy Publishing, 2016).

About the Author

Martha Singleton draws on her experience both as a parent and as one of the country's most respected high school journalism educators.

For forty-two years, she taught various combinations of high school English and journalism, ending with twenty-seven years advising yearbook, news magazine, an online newspaper, and a daily television broadcast at a large inner-city high school in San Antonio.

The University of Texas selected Martha as one of the Top Ten Teachers in Texas, allowing her to participate in education forums with state legislators.

Honored as one of America's Distinguished Journalism Advisers by the Dow Jones Newspaper Fund and the *Wall Street Journal*, she was also given the Edith Fox King Award for service and exemplary teaching by the Interscholastic League Press Conference.

A past president of Texas Association of Journalism Educators, Martha also served on the Texas textbook selection committee, and teaches workshops and seminars for both journalism students and advisers at local, state, and national levels.

In addition to her career as an educator, she has supported her husband in his various positions as youth pastor, music director, and pastor, and now is actively involved as her son pastors a church, and her son-in-law and daughter lead the youth ministry there.

Her children caught her passion for education, and her daughter is the lead theatre teacher and her son is the journalism teacher at the public high school where she taught for twenty-seven years.

Her love for and understanding of both students and their parents, her expertise in educational philosophy and practice and her sense of humor contribute to her ability to share, in an entertaining way, wisdom, faith, and practical advice for parents making decisions concerning their children's education.

NOTES

"We live in a world that is constantly telling us what to love and live for, but in the end we only find ourselves with earthly treasures that do not last. *The View through Your Window* cuts through the cultural noise and provides the necessary tools to develop and live out your family's unique, God-inspired vision. I'm confident many lives will be impacted by this book!"

—**Ryan Gikas,** Pastor of Music & Arts, Bridgeway Church, Oklahoma City, and cofounder of The Verses Project

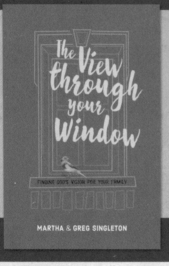

FINDING GOD'S VISION FOR YOUR FAMILY

Martha and Greg Singleton

$14.99

Instead of presenting an impossible standard for our families, God's vision takes into account each individual and acts as an overarching compass that guides individual families on their unique journey of growing together in love and service to Christ. Discover how a God-inspired vision for your family can provide focus, unity, and effectiveness in your day-to-day lives and in your influence on the world around you.

LEAFWOOD
P U B L I S H E R S
an imprint of Abilene Christian University Press

www.leafwoodpublishers.com | 877-816-4455 (toll free)